HIGH PROFIT
FINANCIAL
MANAGEMENT
FOR YOUR SMALL BUSINESS

SUZANNE CAPLAN

DEARBORN™
A **Kaplan Professional** Company

This publication is designed to provide accurate and authoritative information in regard to the subject matter covered. It is sold with the understanding that the publisher is not engaged in rendering legal, accounting, or other professional service. If legal advice or other expert assistance is required, the services of a competent professional person should be sought.

Acquisitions Editor: Robin Nominelli
Managing Editor: Jack Kiburz
Project Editor: Trey Thoelcke
Interior Design: Lucy Jenkins
Cover Design: Scott Rattray, Rattray Design
Typesetting: Elizabeth Pitts

Printed in the United States of America

99   00   01   10   9   8   7   6   5   4   3   2   1

Library of Congress Cataloging-in-Publication Data

Caplan, Suzanne.
    High profit financial management for your small business / Suzanne Caplan.
        p.   cm.
    Includes index.
    ISBN 1-57410-128-5
    1. Small business—Finance.   2. Small business—Management.
    I. Title.
HG4027.7.C3635   1999
658.15'92—dc21   99-16668
                                                                                      CIP

Dearborn books are available at special quantity discounts to use as premiums and sales promotions, or for use in corporate training programs. For more information, please call the Special Sales Manager at 800-621-9621, ext. 4514, or write to Dearborn Financial Publishing, Inc., 155 North Wacker Drive, Chicago, IL 60606-1719.

Dedication

To Mildred Caplan, my mother, who taught me the value of being practical.

Contents

Preface

There are vast numbers of business owners, operating companies with revenues in the millions, who don't have a clue about successful financial management. I know because I was one of them. I spent years running a manufacturing plant by instinct. I "sort of" knew my costs; I "kind of" knew what price the market would bear; and I tried to make those two produce a healthy bottom line. Some years I was very successful and some years not, and I was never quite sure why. If this describes your tenure as CEO, don't be embarrassed: you have plenty of company. I see your "twins" every day in my consulting practice and in my seminars.

You can change this weakness into a strength, however, without getting a degree in accounting—I've never even taken a formal class in the subject. I had a mentor—my banker, Tom Nunnally. Early in my business career, he taught me how to read a balance sheet and financial statement and how to do pro formas (samples) of these for my own business. I must admit that I was a slow learner. I was lucky that he was a patient teacher.

Now that I have mastered some of the financial skills, however, there is no doubt that I feel more in control of my environment. I certainly make more effective use of my accountant, now that I understand what he is saying. And I know where to look when

I'm not satisfied with my results and where to go for profitable new business. Once I admitted my own financial naiveté and corrected it, I was on the road to greater knowledge of how a business does and should work—a valuable skill!

I have written this book in everyday English, not the financial jargon used by those often called the "bean counters." You should not only read it through but more important, keep it as a resource.

Knowledge is power: learn about what to do in many different financial circumstances and you will be prepared to make informed decisions. Some of the sections may not apply to you today, but they will describe situations you may face at some point in the life of your business. There is a beginning, a middle, and an end to all ventures.

This book will help whether you are at the start of your business, building a strong foundation; the middle, trying to keep it vibrant and profitable; in a bit of difficulty trying to solve problems; or planning for a successful exit.

Actually, numbers are fun. They keep score and give you instant feedback on how your business is doing. Numbers don't lie. And plotting a financial strategy is an exciting challenge. Use your banker or accountant as your mentor to build your financial muscles.

I welcome your comments, suggestions, and even questions—which I will try to answer. Contact me at:

Suzanne Caplan
PMB 212
2927 West Liberty Avenue
Pittsburgh, PA 15216
Or e-mail me at suzcaplan@aol.com.

Acknowledgments

I would never have completed my first book—or any other for that matter—had it not been for the professional work of Sherry Truesdell. You are the best! And my agent, Laurie Harper, is a gift for her insight, advice, and professional expertise.

To the professionals I have worked with—Alan Cech, Mike Monaco, and Tom Nunnally—I have learned much from you. To my level-headed friends—Norm Belt, Mark Bibro, Debbie and Don Phillips, Jeff Cowan, and Vera Auretto—I value your contributions to my life and to my work. To my great clients—the Wilsons; the Kims; the Connelleys; Larry Felder, Mickey Schnakenberg, and Dana Shuster; and Lisa Tealer—I appreciate your confidence in me. To my editor, Robin Nominelli, you are a pleasure to work with on every level.

Thanks to the reviewers—Mildred Holley of the University of Arkansas–Little Rock SBDC; Neil Lerner of the University of Wisconsin–Madison SBDC; James O'Connell of the Connecticut SBDC; and Jimmie Wilkins of Chemeketa Community College (Oregon) SBDC—who provided excellent suggestions that were implemented into the final manuscript.

And finally, to my heroes at the Small Business Development Centers throughout the United States: your contribution to the success of small business is undeniable and far too unheralded. I salute you.

Introduction

The entrepreneurial life is an exciting one. Starting a new business is a creative and challenging way to work, and the rewards may well be substantial. Many of us are first motivated to start our own business by a product or service that we find very interesting, or a talent for marketing and sales that seems to translate most effectively in a small business environment. Few entrepreneurs come from a background of accounting and finance, even though this discipline and skill is most critical to the success of any venture. For those less inclined to this discipline, the answer is *not* to hire an outsider and then delegate all of the "number crunching" while keeping your distance from that aspect of business management. Nor is it to find inside controllers and pay little or no attention to what they do and the reports they generate. Too many businesspeople make this choice, which almost always turns out to be a mistake because you end up with no yardstick with which to measure your success (or failure).

You do not have to perform the day-to-day recordkeeping, or even understand all of the mechanical aspects of your accounting system. You should, however, have a good working knowledge of how to read and interpret your financial reports. After all, business is about competition, and these reports are the ones that represent the score. You won't know how you are doing unless you can read your own financials, primarily your balance sheet and profit and loss statement. The more knowledgeable you become, the more you will be able to make decisions that enhance your bottom line. After all, profits are the purpose of the enterprise. Profits are the result of solid business basics such as proper pricing, effective budgeting, and diligent cost control. The information you require to successfully meet all of these goals is found in the financial records that are generated internally or externally by the accounting functions.

The more you learn about this aspect of your business, the more successful you will be. The earlier in the life of your company you take charge of your financials, the easier your business life will be.

Adequate capital (start-up money) and cash flow (getting paid in a timely fashion) not only make any company far easier and even less stressful to operate, but they increase your options to further enhance your success. If you have periodically experienced a cash crunch, or you have done business with companies that are dealing with painful financial realities, you know how crisis affects your working relationships. Customers who can't pay you on a timely basis strain your ability to continue doing business, at least in part because you can't pay your suppliers—who may then choose not to supply you.

The time to begin a good financial strategy is before your doors even open. You must have a complete and detailed understanding of your business start-up costs. At the beginning you need to pay legal and accounting fees, rent, equipment, inventory, insurance coverage, etc. And then there is the critical issue of working capital—some necessary to finance early losses and some to fund operating expenses such as salaries and utilities while cash flow catches up with sales. This book will help you understand and create a comprehensive budget that includes a pro forma profit and loss statement and cash flow projection.

Another aspect of a successful start-up is finding adequate capital from the best source. We will look at all of the alternatives such as equity and debt capital and assess their pros and cons. You must launch your venture on the right foot.

Your operating patterns are set early in your business life. You need to decide how to reach people who want to buy products like yours, and then convince them that of all the choices, they should choose you. Additionally, customers are always looking for value—what they get for their money. The higher the perceived value, the more you can charge. Your costs of doing business, external market conditions, and the marketing decisions you make to secure a profitable piece of the market, will affect your pricing decisions. Add knowledge of production and operations and the costs related to these issues. You'll learn how to balance all these factors to have a strong company.

Once past the early stage of operations, most new companies focus their energy and resources to growing to the size that will secure future profitability. To do that, you must find your break-even point—the volume of sales you require to begin to be profitable. This is another accounting-based analysis that will help you reach your goals if you understand and use it.

Budgeting is another critical element in controlling costs. It too is based on financial assumptions. Most business projections—whether profit and loss, or cash flow, are part science and part art. This book will show you the technical part. You will add to the mix the part that is based on your own product and/or market knowledge.

Growth must be fueled by the timely availability of outside capital—usually a bank loan that meets your financial needs in both amount and terms. Your ability to secure the right financing will be determined by the degree to which you can persuade a lender that your loan proposal is reasonable and the business strategy you are pursuing is viable. It will be the financial records that you submit as back-up documentation that will be a major key to whether or not your loan application is successful. Even if you have reports prepared by an outside professional, you must be ready to discuss them with your banker; we will show you how. And this book will discuss ways to expand a modest, but innovative, venture into a large operation using strategic alliances, partnerships, and/or public ownership to finance its expansion.

A mature business needs effective monitoring and management to keep it operating smoothly and profitably. This book will show you what trends to watch and how to spot the signs of trouble in their early stages, which is the best way to prevent more serious problems.

We will present a strategic plan to turn around a business that may have drifted off course, whether only slightly or more seriously. Understanding the financial implications of your decisions will allow you to exercise more control so you can effect a good outcome. Decision making methods will be presented in a way that facilitates understanding and implementation by even those owners without extensive formal financial backgrounds. Careful reading of this book will allow you to master the necessary skills.

For the times when your company is enjoying success and positive cash flow, several recommendations will be made to enhance your cash position by putting your money to work for you. Good money management in your good times will help you weather the lean times. Consistently monitoring your finances is a constant thread of your business life.

Ultimately, your goal is not just to create a successful business, but to enjoy the benefits of your hard work. You must think about the future of the company, whether it is a family-owned operation with succession in place, a business that must be sold to an outsider, or an enterprise that must be liquidated. Preparing for a smooth transition is the final step to your own successful business career. How to prepare the company, as well as yourself, for the transition is the starting place for this phase of your learning.

Your next step is to find a buyer and negotiate a successful deal and then, ultimately, to be paid on time and in full.

Few entrepreneurs are drawn into business for purely financial reasons. A spirit of independence and a bent towards creativity are important attributes that drive people to become self-employed. And while monetary rewards may be a factor, success isn't always measured in financial terms—other forms of accomplishment are valued as well.

Financial problems, whether chronic and nagging, or acute and severe, will undermine even the most talented and tenacious business owner. Few companies escape periodic difficulties such as pressures on profitability or short-term cash flow shortages. The critical element in overcoming these challenges is knowing how to see the signs early on and where to look to find the solutions.

Your basic financial documents—a complete profit and loss statement, balance sheet, and cash flow projections—are the beginning point. Determining important trends by understanding key ratios will give you the insight to make changes where needed and focus attention on the critical areas that require change. You will feel more in control and be a better leader when you are confident about the direction you are taking the company. The financial professionals you work with inside of the company in your own accounting department as well as your outside accountants and even your banker will be better utilized and their performance enhanced due to your increased participation. After all, you bring the other disciplines into the mix: understanding of market conditions and sales potential and skills at production and operations. Combined with solid financial management, this is a winning business team.

And finally, believe it or not, once you learn the jargon and comprehend the intricacies, financial management is both interesting and challenging. Contrary to what you may have believed, this is a vibrant part of the business as well, and one where skill breeds success.

We end this work with an easy-to-understand glossary of the financial terms used by accountants, bankers, and other "numbers" people. You must learn the language to communicate better. From the time you create your company to the time it passes from your hands, if you learn to plan your finances, outthink your competition, and play defense as well as offense in marketing and pricing policies, you are likely to come out a winner!

Your Financial Toolbox

*You're riding high in April, shot down in May. But I know
I'm gonna change that tune when I'm back on top in June.
That's life.*

*—Dean Kay Thompson and Kelly Gordon,
recorded by Frank Sinatra, Oct. 1966*

Learning Objectives

Once you have completed this chapter, you will be able to:

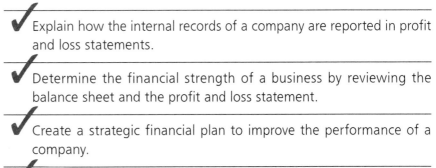

✔ Explain how the internal records of a company are reported in profit and loss statements.

✔ Determine the financial strength of a business by reviewing the balance sheet and the profit and loss statement.

✔ Create a strategic financial plan to improve the performance of a company.

✔ Determine the current rate of return generated by a company.

✔ Explain the breakeven analysis and how to change that number to maintain or increase profits.

There are a number of basic financial instruments that you must learn to read and comprehend as the starting point of gaining financial understanding. These documents, which start with the profit and loss statement and the balance sheet, may be generated in your office by an accounting software program, or your accountant may provide them. Many entrepreneurs give these reports a casual glance, looking at the top line (total volume) and hopefully scrutinizing the bottom line (profit). Many of us, if our accountant or banker does not point out some problem, do not give these reports in-depth analysis, and that is where the financial insight is found. There are key numbers to watch and trends to chart, and you should be aware of what they are and how you can use them.

The Profit and Loss Statement

The simplified explanation of this report is that it tells you how much money you have gained (or lost) from operating your company. But in reality, a profit and loss statement tells you far more than that. The report allocates all of your expenses to specific categories, determined by where the numbers are posted in your general ledgers (called the company's "books"). The posting is governed by a numerical list referred to as the chart of accounts.

What Is the Chart of Accounts?

This chart is a good place to start to explain the details of how a profit and loss statement is constructed. The numbering system is created by acceptable accounting principles. The details are customized by each business, and this is the starting point of your participation. The established numbers run from 100 (or 1,000) to 800 (or 8,000), and some or all of the numbers in any category may be used. The numbered categories are as follows:

100 Assets

Current assets—cash, accounts receivable, and inventory—are listed under 100–149.

Fixed assets, such as machinery, equipment, and real estate, fall under 150–199.

200 Liabilities

Current liabilities, such as accounts payable, taxes due, wages due, and the current portion of any loan (any amount due within one year), are numbered 200–249.

Long-term liabilities, such as mortgages or the longer term balance of any loan, are listed under 250–299.

300 Equity Account

Owners equity (the difference between assets and liabilities) will be listed in this account, except for retained earnings.

400 Retained Earnings

Retained earnings are profits earned by the business that are not distributed as dividends, but held by the company as capital. Only corporations retain earnings; proprietorships and partnerships pass through profits to owners.

500 Income

This account contains all monies received by the company other than those that are equity investments (which becomes part of the capital base) or loans. This category is where you can create detail that will give you information that is important as a management tool. If your products or services are diverse, you may want to know exactly how much revenue (or sales) you have in each category. It is an excellent way to show trends and a way to determine profitability of a specific product or service you provide.

Look over your chart and customize the numbers any way you want; they can always be modified.

600, 700, 800 Expenses

Establish separate expense account numbers for those costs that are direct (labor and material, or finished product—also referred to as "cost of goods sold") and those that are overhead (or indirect) such as rent, utilities, insurance, and administrative expense including the cost of sales and marketing. Where you post (allocate) an expense will determine where it appears on your profit and loss statement.

How a Profit and Loss Statement Is Reported

The items posted on your company's books are reflected in the income and expense columns of your profit and loss statement. The two line items that most business owners want to see are the total revenue and the profit. But the real story is carried in the lines in between. Typically a statement looks like the one on the following page, although the amount of detail can vary greatly.

No doubt the income number (total sales) is one that interests and concerns you. And it should. Your total volume is important because you need the profits it generates to cover overhead expenses. If you have divided your sales numbers into categories that effectively reflect your sales, you also can see clearly what products or services are selling well and in what areas volume has fallen off. This information is critical to your planning and your budgeting.

Income from operations
   Less returns and credits
      Net sales

Less cost of goods sold
   Products (inventory)
   Labor
      Gross profit

Less general and administrative expense
   Salaries, Officers
   Salaries, Administration
   Salaries, Sales
   Rent
   Utilities
   Phone
   Postage/freight
   Office expenses
   Sales and marketing costs
   Repairs and maintenance
   Auto expense
   Interest expense
   Miscellaneous

      Net (before tax) profit (or loss)

What you really want to concern yourself with in terms of your profit and loss statement is both the direct (or variable) costs and the indirect (or fixed costs). The direct costs are listed first and are often referred to as "cost of goods sold." After they have been deducted from income, what remains is called your gross or operating profit. These costs are referred to as variable because they vary depending on the volume of sales. The more you sell, the more inventory or labor you use. When sales go down, these costs go down as well. Your gross profit margin is very important to understand and control because this gives you a guideline as to how you should be pricing your products/services. An in-depth look at pricing is included in Chapter 4.

Once you know what percentage of mark up you need and what the market will support, then you will be able to go after new business *and* make sure it is profitable. You will take your direct costs and add your predetermined percentage to it.

If you see your gross margin going down, it is likely caused by one or both of two possible problems:

1. You have not raised prices sufficiently to cover the cost of material or finished goods.
2. If your labor has gone up as a percentage of costs, it may be due to lowered productivity—either mechanical or human. You need to investigate the reason. If the problem is mechanical, you may need to update your technology. If the problem is human, you may need to retrain or motivate your workforce. If neither is the problem, or the problem is uncorrectable, you may need to adjust your selling price or live with lower profits.

Next, turn your attention to fixed or indirect costs. These costs—such as rent, telephone, insurance—continue no matter how much volume you do. You must keep sales at a level high enough to generate sufficient gross profits to cover these expenses, plus leave a net profit.

Your overhead costs should be monitored as a form of control—each one should have a limit not only in dollars but in percentage of total sales. The more your sales grow, the more you can—but do not have to—allocate to line items such as marketing and promotional expense, travel, and entertainment. Hiring decisions for support staff also must be made with serious consideration to their cost as a percentage of sales. All expenses should be reviewed as a percentage of sales.

The following is a look at a profit and loss statement (P&L) for a construction company. Its direct costs are material, labor doing the actual construction (along with union fringe benefit payments), and subcontractors. The indirect (fixed overhead) costs are all other costs. All costs are expressed in percentages.

Mac Construction, Inc.
Profit and Loss Statement
Year ending December 31, 1999

	In dollars	As percentage
Fees	$1,500,000	100.0
Cost of sales		
Direct labor	450,000	30.0
Union benefits	150,000	10.0
Material costs	360,000	24.0
Subcontractors	45,000	3.0
Total cost of sales	1,005,000	67.0
Gross profit	495,000	33.0
Expenses (overhead and G&A)		
Accounting expense	7,500	.5
Auto and truck	45,000	3.0
Bad debt expense	–0–	–0–
Insurance	90,000	6.0
Interest	9,000	.6
Legal and professional advice	3,600	.3
Office salaries	45,000	3.0
Officer salary	90,000	6.0
Payroll tax	60,000	4.0
Rent	30,000	2.0
Telephone	9,000	.6
Travel	4,500	.3
Utilities	7,500	.5
Miscellaneous	15,000	1.0
Total expense	416,100	28.8
Net (before tax) profit	$ 78,900	4.2

You will use your P&L to compare one period to another. Look at your total expense as a percentage for a current period as opposed to the same period last year. Has it gone up or down? If it has grown as a percentage, is that due to actual dollar costs or because the revenue is down and the fixed expenses are taking a greater proportion? If you are going to operate efficiently, you must know what your numerical goals are and be able to track how you are meeting those goals. Trends are important business barometers.

You must know whether your P&L has been done on a cash basis or an accrual basis. This makes a good bit of difference in how you will read and interpret the data. A cash basis statement shows a transaction *only* when the cash actually changes hands (payment of receivables). A sale will be reported as income only when the money is received, not when the sale is made. An expense is only recorded when it is paid for, not when it is incurred. This is a method that works best for primarily cash businesses such as restaurants. If you allow customers to buy on credit and purchase your needs on credit as well, you will not get as accurate a reading from a cash basis statement because you are unlikely to be able to match income and expense in the same period.

Accrual basis is the method where income is earned even if the cash has not been received, and expenses are accounted for when they occur, whether paid for or not. You will create accounts for money owed you as well as for money you owe. The revenue and expense will normally match for a given period, allowing you to accurately judge how you are doing for any given period. An accrual basis accounting system is more complicated and time consuming but often worth the effort because the results are far more accurate and useful. With software or professionally prepared P&Ls, they are easy to produce, but you must understand what they really are telling you.

Profits or Losses Are Reflected on the Balance Sheet

Another one of the important financial documents generated by your company is your balance sheet, which shows you the current financial strength of the business. This report lists the assets and liabilities of your company and shows your current net worth (assets minus liabilities). As with your profit and loss statement, your chart of accounts will determine the categories that are listed as detail in your balance sheet.

A typical balance sheet is set up as follows:

Assets
    Current assets
        Cash and cash items
        Accounts receivable
        Notes receivable—short-term (12 months or less)
        Inventory
    Fixed assets
        Land and buildings
        Machinery and equipment
          (Less depreciation)
        Long-term notes receivable (more than 1 year)
            Total assets

Liabilities
    Current liabilities
        Accounts payable
        Accrued wages (earned but not paid)
        Payroll taxes due
        Loans due (current portion—less than 12 months)
            Total current liabilities
    Long-term liabilities
        (Portions of notes or loans due beyond current 12-month period)
            Total liabilities

Stockholders equity (total assets minus total liabilities)

Here's the balance sheet for our case study construction company.

Mac Construction, Inc.
Balance Sheet
December 31, 1999

Current assets

Cash and cash items	$ 18,500	
Accounts receivable	285,000	
Inventory, material	50,000	
Prepaid insurance	12,000	
Work in progress	31,000	
Utility deposits	1,000	
Total		$397,500
Machinery and equipment	45,000	
Less depreciation	30,000	
Total		15,000
Total assets		412,500

Current labilities

Accounts payable	118,000	
Sales tax payable	9,200	
401K deductions	1,400	
Union benefits	6,400	
N/P—Chase Bank	21,000	
Total current liabilities		156,000

Long-term liabilities

Chase Bank (noncurrent)	142,000	
Total liabilities		298,000
Capital		
Common stock	10,000	
Retained earnings	114,500	
Total stockholders equity		$124,500

Understand Your Net Worth

Stockholders equity is also referred to as net worth. An important point to remember is that this is the book value of the business, which is the tangible assets less the depreciation. First, only the real property is accounted for. This is the machinery, equipment, and buildings (if they are owned by the business), plus cash, accounts receivable, and inventory. Only some of the intangible property—such as the value of licenses, trademarks, patents, and franchise rights—are included. Intellectual property and other intangibles such as the value of the company name are not accounted for on the books but they can add value to the worth of the business.

In addition, the depreciation schedule used may either overstate or understate the true current value of your assets. For example, a piece of equipment may be fully depreciated on your books in seven years, but at the end of that time, it may still have thousands of dollars of resale value. Because of standard accounting practices, this will not show as a part of your net worth. On the other hand, computer equipment may still have value on your books but in reality, be obsolete. Don't take your balance sheet on face value; take a deeper look to determine your company's real worth.

Remember to adjust for inventory that is no longer usable or saleable and must be written off, and for accounts receivable that are uncollectible. These items, while they may still be on your books, are really not assets at all. Make sure you or your accountant makes annual adjustments to these line items.

The Test of Solvency

Solvency is the ability to pay your debts from your current cash flow. Your balance sheet will give you a fairly accurate picture as to how likely you are to be able to retire current debts using the normal cash flow generated by current assets. You determine your solvency using what is known as current ratios. You determine this ratio by comparing current assets to current liabilities. First, there must be more current assets than current debts, but even if the number is equal or nearly so, you may have problems. Unsaleable inventory or uncollectible receivables that never turn to cash could be the source of your serious cash flow problems. A 2-to-1 ratio is safe (twice as many assets as liabilities), but a 3-to-2 ratio may be sufficient. A safe ratio depends on the normal turnover of your inventory and the collection cycle of your receivables.

Look back at the balance sheet of Mac Construction to perform a solvency test. Only cash and accounts receivable are liquid enough to be used as current assets for this purpose. They total $303,500. Current liabilities total $156,000. This is a 2-to-1 ratio and this business passes the solvency requirements easily.

A balance sheet should be reviewed in depth at least quarterly (the end of a three-month period) to take the financial pulse of the business. An annual in-depth review should compare current figures with previous years. Then you can tell if you are building or losing equity and liquidity in the business. If you see no improvement, this is a sign that positive action is required. Go back to your profit and loss statement to look at current levels of profitability and determine what can be done to improve it, which will improve the balance sheet as well.

Reading Your Cash Flow Statement

You can determine your degree of solvency from your balance sheet, but you must create a cash flow statement to predict how easily you can retire obligations from your current level of income. This is the way to determine if a loan is required to meet higher variable costs due to a period of growth or increased sales, or if a loan already on your books is going to present a problem to repay in the immediate future.

A cash flow statement differs from your profit and loss statement in a number of ways such as:

- Depreciation which is deducted from profit (for tax purposes) is a noncash item and does not show on a cash flow statement.
- Only the interest portion of your loan is on a profit and loss statement because principal is not deductible from your taxable income. The principal payment, however, still must be paid from the available cash, so it is shown on a cash flow projection.

You must remember as you create this statement that cash received is not the same as revenue if sales are made on a credit basis. It may take as little as 30 days for the turn to cash or as long as 90 days, and you must account for this.

A cash flow statement is formatted as follows:

```
Starting cash (monies left from previous period)
  +          Revenue (cash sales and collection of receivables)
  +          proceeds from loans
  +          sales of assets or additional investment
  +          additional owner capital
  _____

  =          Total cash available


  –          Direct expense
  –          Operating expense (without depreciation)
  –          Debt service (including principal payment)
  _____

  =          Ending cash (the starting cash for next period)
```

Managing cash flow is a critical skill for any business owner. It becomes even more important during (1) times of growth and (2) the periods when cash collections slow down, which is often the case at the end of the year and at tax time. The growth cycle, however, remains the greatest challenge. How do you fund greater expenses that come along with increased sales before your cash collections catch up? This often requires outside funds for use as working capital. A cash flow projection will tell you how much you need and for how long. A shortfall in cash flow can stop a growth period in its tracks because you won't be able to buy material or product to handle new orders. It can even undermine the stability of the operation as a whole because inability to supply your customers allows competitors to steal them. Learn to do the pro formas so that you can predict what's going to happen and hopefully take steps to lessen its effects by arranging adequate cash flow.

In some business instances, the primary one being a cash business such as a service company or a restaurant, funding growth is less difficult. You can fund your growth with cash received as you go along. In another scenario, your vendor credit increases as sales rise and, in reality, your supplier is funding your growth. Not a bad deal for them if their sales to your company increase as well. There are other techniques for supplementing cash requirements to fund growth (see Chapter 5), but you must start by knowing how much cash or cash equivalent you will need. A pro forma cash flow statement will give you this information.

Know the Difference between Cash Flow and Profit

Cash flow and profit are not the same thing and you should understand the difference. It is possible to be operating a profitable business and still have cash flow problems. Some of the causes are growth, slow collections, and high debt service. The interest on debt is deductible so it comes off the profit and loss statement, but if the terms of your loans are short and the principal payments are high, the total debt service may cause an ongoing cash crunch. To alleviate this, seek a restructuring of your loan to extend the payout period. If the business is profitable otherwise, most lenders will cooperate.

A high cash business such as a restaurant may have good cash flow but be losing money. If you are getting money today and deferring expenses (payroll, taxes, vendor payments) until a week or a month from now, you will hide your problems in the cash flow for a while. Ultimately, if you are losing money from operations, the cash flow will not be sufficient to meet obligations, and losses will mount. Watch both of these indicators.

Profit will ultimately add to cash flow as you build a working capital base by retaining earnings. Another way to smooth out cash flow is to have a line of credit from your lender that you can draw on when cash gets tight. A line of credit may be drawn on as needed and paid back as cash begins to flow better. It is similar to having a reserve account, and better than a term loan. With a term loan, you are paying interest for money you don't need now and may never need.

Working with a Breakeven Analysis

This report will tell you what gross sales volume you need at the current level of profitability in order to break even, which, of course, is the starting point to making a profit. This report is not normally created by most accountants or company controllers and does not automatically generate with small business accounting software. You must ask for it, but it is a highly recommended report for you to have, to understand, and to utilize. If you are just beginning your business, this number is an important projection. Until you reach the breakeven volume, you will lose money, and these losses will have to be funded by your working capital. For the first few years, you can use a breakeven to measure how you are doing against earlier projections. Once your company has become a mature business, you still must review your current breakeven to find out if you have allowed expenses to creep up or margins to drop, which increases the volume required and lowers profits.

General and Administrative Expense (monthly)	
Officer's salaries	$ 5,000
Office wages	1,800
Rent	1,200
Utilities	500
Insurance	500
Telephone	600
Auto expense	400
Sales and marketing	1,200
Travel and entertainment	1,000
Interest	500
Miscellaneous	1,000
Total expense	$13,700

You can lower your breakeven and increase your bottom line if you understand what your breakeven number is. It is the volume level where, after direct costs are accounted for, the gross profit dollars are sufficient to cover the fixed or indirect costs. Your fixed costs should always include the monthly portion of any expenses, even if they are paid on an annual basis. Items in this category may include insurance premiums and quarterly tax. Look at the following simple budget of overhead expense for a hypothetical business to see how to figure a breakeven.

You must generate sufficient volume at your current gross profit margin to generate $13,700 in operating profits. Let's assume that your direct costs of material (raw material or inventory) and labor (production, service, etc.) are 30 percent of sales. Your breakeven volume would be at slightly less than $20,000—30 percent of that is $6,000 direct costs, which leaves your gross profit at $14,000, which is sufficient to cover your overhead at $13,700.

Breakeven Volume Can Be Changed

The two critical numbers here are your gross profit margins and your fixed expense. Neither of these are numbers etched in stone. Most business owners look at their breakeven as a volume-driven number, and for some it is. When sales go up and get beyond this trigger point, profits follow: the higher the sales, the higher the profit. But there are situations where you may not be able to increase volume sufficiently. For example:

- You have reached good market penetration and without additional products or services to provide, growth is temporarily stopped.
- Your current production capacity has been met, and you cannot generate more product at this time, even if you have the demand. New capital investment is required and profitability must be restored before money is available. What are the strategies?
  1. Lower your direct costs and raise the gross margin. Perhaps the savings can be found in better purchasing, finding bargains, or selling a greater portion of your inventory at full price. Have you been diligent about monitoring these?

     The other part of direct costs is labor. You can increase productivity by better use of new technology and maximizing the scheduling and use of workers. Make sure you have as little downtime as possible and keep your labor force as lean as possible.
  2. Use strict controls on overhead expense and lower the costs. Some of these costs may be very flexible, such as marketing and travel. Make sure you don't pull back so far that future sales are jeopardized. Office expenses should be watched. If costs, such as insurance, seem to be getting too high, solicit new bids. Employee benefits may grow without anyone being fully aware of how much they are increasing because per-employee coverage remains the same. In serious cases, you may need to

lower your rent through negotiation or moving your office, or officers' salaries must be cut back to stem the losses. You know the realistic volume levels and you know the flexibility of your direct costs—so this may be the place you need to start.

3. Now may be the time to raise prices. We will do an in-depth analysis in Chapter 4 on the effect of pricing. You will be surprised at how great an impact it can have. Most small business owners are reluctant to increase pricing for fear that they will lose business. A nominal raise of 3 percent to 4 percent will tend to be pure profit and will decrease your breakeven substantially so you can afford to lose a bit of volume. Chances are you won't. You will likely find that your customers are not that price conscious when doing business with a small company. They patronize you for other reasons, such as quality, flexibility, and personalized service. Price sensitive customers go to volume companies.

Look at the effect of a 4 percent price increase. This would lower your $20,000 gross volume breakeven to a shade under $18,000 breakeven—a 10 percent reduction. No one wants to lose sales, but if your volume dropped 5 percent—which really is quite a lot—you would still have more profit through higher pricing. You may want to enhance some of your services or change your product mix to raise the perception of value as you institute any new pricing.

The Next Tools Are Known as Ratios

There are ways of measuring your company's performance and determining the direction of its progress. Called ratios, these measurements are numerical calculations that will show you critical benchmark information about your business. Financial analysts such as those working with your lender may use more than a dozen different ratios to review a business. You will only need to do five or six, but be prepared to monitor them regularly. You are looking for any trends that deviate from the norms of your own industry. And you are looking for period-to-period comparisons to track your direction and enhance what appears to be working and take corrective action where there are signs of an unwanted downward direction.

The first ratio we already reviewed is the "current ratio," which is calculated from your balance sheet. This measures your liquidity by determining whether current assets are sufficient to pay current liabilities in a timely manner.

For example, a business with $10,000 in cash, $60,000 in accounts receivable, and $50,000 in inventory has $120,000 of current assets. On the other side, if it has $45,000 of accounts payable and $15,000 in current (payable in 12 months or less) loan obligations, its current liabilities are $60,000, giving it a 2-to-1 current ratio, which is within the desirable range. The one caution here is to be honest about how much inventory is not saleable and what percentage of your receivables are not collectible. If the total amount is negligible, you are fine, but if you know that 25 percent of each are in the questionable range, you must pay attention to that. If the $110,000 worth of inventory and receivables we just described are reduced by $27,500 (25 percent), then current assets are down to $93,500 and your ratio is 1.5-to-1, which is far more problematic. Pay attention to this ratio and be honest in your assessment of your condition.

The Quick Ratio

If you aren't sure how much of your inventory is obsolete, or you typically move your inventory very slowly, there is a version of the current ratio that may work for you. Here you will drop the inventory totally from the asset side and count cash and accounts receivable only. From the 2-to-1 ratio that you may have expected on the typical current ratio, an acceptable level for a quick ratio may be as low as 1.3-to-1 (you must have $130 worth of assets for each $100 worth of liabilities). The faster your receivables collect, the closer you can get this margin.

Debt-to-Worth Ratio

You will determine this number by dividing your total debt (all long-term and short-term debt) by your total equity (the bottom line on your balance sheet). For example, if your debt is $200,000 and your equity is $100,000, your debt-to-equity ratio is 2-to-1. Most lenders like to see it at 3-to-1 or below, so this level is very acceptable.

This ratio measures the leverage you are using—how you are putting your equity to work to generate additional capital for the ongoing operation.

The start-up and early phases of most businesses are fueled by debt. Optimally, operating costs will soon be met from current profit. If the ratio remains high or begins to grow, it could be dangerous. Lenders may refuse to extend further credit (on which the company is operating) and a cash crunch could occur.

Inventory Turnover Ratio

You should know how many times your inventory turns over (or sells). If it is too slow, you may have too much of your money tied up in inventory. This ratio is derived from the annual "material" costs of goods sold divided by the ending inventory. As an example, if you have had $500,000 of material costs and you currently have $100,000 of products on hand, then your inventory turns five times a year. Divide that into 365 days and you now know your inventory turns every 73 days.

You must watch how the days change, whether they go up or down. Cash flow shortages very often begin with slowing inventory turnover. If you must pay your vendors in 30 days but it takes you 73 days to sell your product, you can easily see how trouble begins.

Payable Turnover Ratio

The total volume of all of your purchases is divided by your current accounts payable. As an example, you purchase $600,000 annually and your current payables are $150,000—that gives you a ratio of 4. Divide 4 into 365 to get 91; this is how many days it takes you to pay a bill. If this were your situation, it would probably mean that your business is having cash flow problems because most vendors want to be paid in 45 days or sooner. You must carefully watch this.

It is possible, even desirable, to use vendor credit as a low interest (usually no interest) loan to finance your cash flow by taking longer to pay, even though this means paying interest on the amount due. Unless you are being given discount terms for prompt payment and have the available cash, you may want to time your payables between 30 and 50 days.

Receivable Turnover Ratio

This number is calculated by dividing your annual sales by your current total receivables. For example, if your annual volume is $1,000,000 and your current accounts receivable are $200,000, then you turn inventory five times a year. Divide 365 by 5 to get a turnover time of 73 days. This means that a sale you make on credit on January first will not get paid on average until the middle of March. Unless you set up your pro formas to reflect that payment schedule, it will create cash flow problems.

You must pay wages and overhead for two months before you realize the cash from your sale. You can see the pressure reflected in a deteriorating payable ratio.

You will need your receivable ratio to show you how to project revenue in your cash flow statement. If you have sales in January that don't collect until March, that is when the cash will be available for your use. As sales go up, costs of selling go up, and cash gets tighter.

You must be diligent about collecting your receivables. Your turnover ratio will measure your success at this effort. When the days go down, it shows success and makes operations much easier from a cash management standpoint.

Return on Equity Ratio

This number is found by dividing the net equity (bottom line on balance sheet) by the net profit earned by the company. For instance, if your equity is $250,000 and last year you earned a profit of $50,000, then your return is 20 percent. This is the way you can decide if your investment is working for you or if you would be better off selling out and putting the cash somewhere else. Money invested in a small business is always at risk, so, like other investments, the higher the risk, the larger the return you should expect. Don't forget to consider in this the amount of compensation and benefits you receive that may be divided for ownership as opposed to wages.

Return on Assets Ratio

This is determined by dividing the total assets by the net profit earned. If your assets total $500,000 and you earned a net profit of $25,000, your return is 5 percent. If this number goes down, the company is not utilizing assets properly. Perhaps an asset sale is called for if money is invested in nonperforming assets. Often ownership of property falls into this category; a company may sell its plant and rent it back.

Using Measuring Tools

All of these financial tools, from the reports to the ratios, are important barometers of how your business is doing. You must understand them and how to use them. Ways of measuring the progress and the outcome of your business operation are found in the various reports and ratios discussed here. Understanding what these measurements are and what they tell you will take you far in creating and operating a profitable business.

2

The Start-Up

*Without the element of uncertainty, the bringing off
of even the greatest business triumph would be a dull,
routine, and eminently unsatisfying affair.*

—J. Paul Getty

Learning Objectives

Once you have completed this chapter, you will be able to:

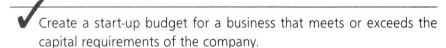

✔ Create a start-up budget for a business that meets or exceeds the capital requirements of the company.

✔ Establish the parameters of a basic accounting system and create financial pro formas that are valuable management tools as well as credible external documents.

✔ Explain various financing alternatives, such as investment capital versus debt capital, and analyze which is most beneficial for your company.

✔ Develop a plan for attracting investment and structuring a reasonable return.

✔ Create a realistic plan for future growth.

The stage is being set for the success of your venture before you even open the doors of your business. Your financial future may be determined by how you prepare yourself financially and how you live up to the financial goals you set while planning your venture. You must research your costs and fully understand all of the elements of your start-up budget and how to stay within the limits you have set. Also, you must plan in advance for the first stage of the business cycle—getting to profitability—so you have the staying power to reach your long-term goal.

How Much Does It Cost to Start a Business?

Starting your business does not just mean having a product or service and enough money to open the doors. Many critical costs may not be obvious to the new business owner, but they must be accounted for. Here's a list of six start-up costs you should review to make sure you have included everything you need.

Start-Up Cost #1

Professional advice, both legal and accounting. Initial fees could be as low as $1,000 or more than $5,000, depending on the complexity of a business organization.

You will have to hire a lawyer to assist you with a number of decisions and filings that all new companies must make, the first decision being the type of legal entity you will become—a corporation, a partnership, or a sole proprietorship. Not every new business needs to be incorporated. That decision should be made on a case-by-case basis. The more complicated the legal entity you create, the more expensive it will be to set up, in the costs of both legal fees and filing fees for government bodies. The cost of filing taxes is higher as well because the tax forms are more complicated.

The question of whether to incorporate or not is usually the basic one. You can go into business as an individual, but the primary risk is that all of the liability the company takes on will also be yours personally. If the company fails, you may have to pay debts from your personal funds. If someone gets a judgment against the company, it could wipe out your personal funds if the company does not have enough money to cover the judgment. One of the main reasons to incorporate is to protect yourself from these possibilities. You may choose a C Corporation, Sub S Corporation, or an LLC (limited liability company). A C Corporation is the model for companies expecting to grow large. Equity investments can be sought publicly for this type of organization. Few small businesses are in a position for a major public offering; if you start as an S Corporation you can always change your legal structure to a C Corporation if the opportunity arises.

Another consideration in your decision of what type of entity to create is a financial one. Do you expect to have substantial losses during the early years? Then it may benefit you to offset other income with these deductions. Meet with an accountant as well to discuss both your expectations and the best way to benefit from your situation. Perhaps the potential for tax deductions would make you attractive to an investor who could transfer them to another enterprise—more about this later in this chapter. Now is the time to get the good advice you will need.

Start-Up Cost #2

Renting and preparing your space, including decorating and installing shop fixtures such as shelving and display cases, and telephone systems. Get estimates! Can you barter your product or service for some or all of these costs?

Chances are good that your landlord will require some sort of a deposit such as a few months' rent plus one month as security. It is often the case that most of the required changes in the space will be done as an incentive to get you to rent, or the cost may be spread out over the term of the lease.

The decorating items such as carpeting and wall covering may be at your expense.

Remember the cost of telecommunications installation, which may be very substantial. The phone company will want a deposit and they will charge for running the line to the building as well as a per line charge for turning on the service. In addition, wiring and the cost of the phone system itself will be at your expense. You may be able to secure a lease for phones. Don't overbuy, but get a system that will grow with you.

Start-Up Cost #3

Machinery, equipment, and inventory. Use leases where possible and be conservative.

Next on your list will be any equipment you require including vehicles, all production machines, tools, cash registers, office computers, and other administrative equipment requirements. You may be able to lease these outright or lease/purchase some or all of these so your cash outlay will be limited to a deposit and the required security deposit.

You will also need an initial starting inventory that will eventually turn into cash but usually must be purchased outright prior to opening, usually using debt financing. Determining how large an initial inventory you need is extremely difficult because it requires not only assumptions about your customers' demand in types of products but some prediction of your volume of sales as well. You do not want to burden yourself with excess inventory to start because if some of your predictions are off, you may have far too much money tied up in this area and be pressured into selling it below your desired profits in order to generate cash flow. Be conservative, but be alert as well. Secure vendor credit as soon as you are in a position to provide the information necessary to begin. Find out how quickly new inventory can be shipped and factor that into your ordering. If you learn that your initial suppliers have delivery problems and you won't be able to restock easily, you may want to look at other vendors or other product lines. A quick flow of merchandise keeps your costs down and your cash flow up.

Vendor credit is desirable because it smoothes the flow of capital, but it is not easy to obtain for any start-up. Assume that your early inventory will be purchased for cash.

Start-Up Cost #4

All of your printed material, including letterhead, business cards, catalogs, and direct mail material. Choose an image (logo) and keep it consistent. Have it checked by a copyright attorney to be sure someone else hasn't registered your company name or logo. Also consider any advertising or sales related expenses.

You must announce your existence to your potential customers by the use of direct mail, print, radio, public cable and commercial television advertising, and marketing materials. Regardless of the medium, these will be part of the up-front costs of your start-up. Each contact will be expressing a piece of information that will help potential customers form an opinion of who your company is and whether they wish to do business with you. It takes effort to create the effect that you want and may require a professional advisor. However, with today's desktop publishing capabilities as well as very complete quick print businesses that are cost effective, you may be able to do much of the work yourself and keep the cost down.

The cost of a "Grand Opening" event should also be included in your budget. There are other selling costs such as travel and entertainment. Will you have to go outside of your locality to make sales? This will be an ongoing cost that will be recovered by the sales revenue and gross profit. However, a start-up must have money put aside for this purpose.

Start-Up Cost #5

The miscellaneous expenses such as deposits, fees, permits, and licenses that a new business may require. Each industry or business type will have its own demands.

Start-up costs that might be considered one-time expense are those license fees and registration fees that may be charged by local and state governments. In addition, you may also have other deposit requirements for your utilities. You will need business insurance for hazard losses (fire, etc.), liability (product or professional), and workers' compensation in case you or any of your employees are injured in a work-related accident. Most new businesses will need up to 25 percent of the first year's premiums just to activate coverage.

Start-Up Cost #6

Operating capital sufficient to sustain the operation until the revenue cash flow becomes positive.

The final start-up cost is adequate capital to fund the early stages of operation. This operating capital is required to supplement the expected revenues you will have from your business. Few new companies have sufficient volume in their early days to breakeven, much less make a profit. You'll need cash on hand to pay your operating costs until your profits are sufficient to continue the operation.

Creating the Start-Up Budget

There are a number of different ways to construct a budget. You might be inclined to start by listing all of the items you think you will need and assigning a cost to them. When you get to your total, then you can run around to all of your sources and try to raise the money. If you are unable to secure all of the financing, then the tendency is to lower the amount of operating capital you think you need because some of those funds will be required at a later time. In fact, this is the wrong way to set up a winning start-up budget.

The best way to construct an effective budget is to use the amount of accessible capital you have as a goal and structure your plans around that number, prioritizing the absolute costs and limiting the more flexible ones so that the dollars will cover costs.

You will require the following:

1. A legal structure
2. A place to locate
3. The tools of your trade
4. Printed materials as sales tools
5. Deposits and fees
6. Operating capital, including wages

Avoid the extras in each category. You need to be looking in the following areas:

Item #2—Location

Can you use less space?

Can you keep your decorating costs as low as possible and improve the space once the business is profitable? (Restaurants and retail operations often go overboard on design.) Especially if your clients don't come to your facility or wouldn't care (truck drivers, etc.), you can be more basic. Phone and computer systems can be basic or sophisticated; maybe the bells and whistles should wait.

Item #3—Equipment and Inventory

Depending on your suppliers—leasing equipment is far less of an immediate cash outlay than purchasing. You need to be conservative in both the type and quantity of equipment you purchase or lease. Consider used vehicles or machines if they are available and won't affect the quality or quantity of your work.

Computers are essential these days to all new businesses but with the technology changing on a daily basis, you can save a great deal of money shopping around and finding a system that may not be cutting edge but is still adequate for your needs. You can always upgrade for a little money. Your list will likely include a fax/copier and Internet access as well as communication equipment including cell phones and pagers.

Perhaps of all the budget items, inventory is one of the most complex because you need to have enough to generate sales but not so much as to strangle cash. Set a fixed dollar figure based on estimated sales and *stick to it*.

Item #4—Marketing Material

Somewhere between the high-priced consultant and the low budget, off-the-shelf material is the quality of the promotional aids you will want to represent your company. The best way to find what you need is old-fashioned research. See if there is material you admire from another company and find out where it was created. Go to a variety of sources, from quick copy and quick printing places to small independent printers. Explain what you feel you need and take quotes. You may be able to use fewer colors and a less expensive but presentable grade of paper. All of these decisions affect the price and can help you keep the cost in budget and the budget reasonable.

Determining Item #6— The Amount of Operating Capital You Will Require

Here is one place where you want to be absolutely sure you have enough money available. The first five line items are easier to adjust, but adequate operating capital is more critical. This is the cash you will need each month to pay the difference between the amount of money you take in and the amount of money you need to pay out to keep the doors open and keep growing until you get to the point where there are profits.

Few businesses make money in their first few months of operation and many do not make money for the first few years. It doesn't matter whether you are large or small, this is a fact of doing business. The reason is simple: until your revenue growth is sufficient to generate enough operating (or gross) profits to meet or exceed overhead, you are below the breakeven line.

Let's assume your overhead costs are $8,000 per month. These include rent, utilities, insurance, salaries, marketing costs, debt service (interest only), plus any other miscellaneous costs you have. The direct costs (material and labor) of your product or the labor cost of your service is 60 percent of your selling price—$6 for each $10 sale. You will need sales of $20,000 per month ($240,000 per year) to breakeven. How long will it take you to get there? If your sales grow each month, you will need less operating capital each month, but you will continue to need some until your monthly *average* is more than $20,000. So if your first year sales look something like the following chart, your operating capital requirements will be the sum total of your shortfall. There is no way around this.

ABC Company will require $52,800 of operating capital to use from the time it opens its doors until the months when it can cover its expenses. This number assumes that once sales reach the $20,000 mark, the volume will stay there. If that is not the anticipated situation, another year's pro forma will have to be created to establish any additional shortfall. This money should be on hand or readily available before the business opens its doors to avoid the crisis of no cash to pay bills. The alternative for ABC would be to find itself $50,000 in debt at the end of its first year, all past due, with a number of creditors demanding money and making threatening noises and cutting off future credit. This is not the way to grow a successful company.

ABC Company—Year 1 Pro Forma Cash Statement

Month	1	2	3	4	5	6	7	8	9	10	11	12	Total
Sales −	4,000	4,000	5,000	6,000	6,000	8,000	8,000	8,000	12,000	12,000	15,000	20,000	108,000
Direct Costs =	2,400	2,400	3,000	3,600	3,600	4,800	4,800	4,800	7,200	7,200	9,000	12,000	64,800
Operating (Gross) Profits	1,600	1,600	2,000	2,400	2,400	3,200	3,200	3,200	4,800	4,800	6,000	8,000	43,200
Overhead expense =	8,000	8,000	8,000	8,000	8,000	8,000	8,000	8,000	8,000	8,000	8,000	8,000	96,000
Shortfall	<6,400>	<6,400>	<6,000>	<5,600>	<5,600>	<4,800>	<4,800>	<4,800>	<3,200>	<3,200>	<2,000>	0	<52,800>

The Risk of Financing a Start-Up with Debt

Starting a new business on debt financing alone is a less than desirable way to go because you will inevitably overburden the new venture with the cost of debt service (interest), which will then increase your short-term cash problems. And even if you wanted to use debt financing, it is almost impossible to secure business financing for a start-up with no equity investment and therefore no collateral. There is good reason for this.

The cost of your start-up is a long-term investment that will have a payback over years in the form of profits that may be returned to the owner or investor as dividends. Unlike a loan that requires some immediate payback, an investment does not show a return until there is sufficient profitability and positive cash flow. The money you need for operating capital is required because in the start-up phase you often cannot pay your overhead from sales income. And that is without any loan payments—debt service would increase the need for cash and further stress the operation. This obstacle could well cripple a new venture or prevent it from acquiring the ability to fund sufficient growth and become as profitable as it has the potential to be.

While often suggested or even recommended as a source of start-up cash, credit card advances or high interest consumer loans have a very high risk attached to them. First, they are expensive and add the burden of paying the owner sufficient salary to pay them back in *after-tax* dollars. And even if the business pays the loan directly, the interest cost is still an added expense.

An additional question about this type of financing (personal loans) is how you will list it on the balance sheet. If you call it your investment, then it becomes the equity of the company and the payments must be made by you in after-tax dollars. If you list it as a loan payable (either to stockholders, if you have incorporated, or to the lending institution), you now are showing a company that has already acquired some debt without making any profit. Consider how that looks to a banker or investor down the road whom you might ask to provide additional capital to finance the growth phase or to take advantage of a good short-term opportunity. You may not be able to get to the next level of success because of decisions you made early in the game.

There will always be some financial pressure on the small business operator, whether resulting from a sudden drop in sales (and cash) due to some temporary external force such as weather, or from the slow payment of a large creditor. Decisions are always required on how to allocate limited financial resources—paying vendors or landlords, or even at times your own salary. Any lender, whether paid by you or by the company, must be paid on time or there will be a mark on your personal credit or the company's credit. This may have a long-term effect not only in the short-term life of the business, but on your credit rating as well, which will prevent future financing. Your personal credit is often considered as one criteria in a business loan.

One highly promoted loan, called a "business loan" by some banks, is in reality a home equity loan or a second mortgage on your home. The loan value is linked to the equity value in your property and is secured by the home itself. Take caution before deciding to go this route because new businesses are always a risk—a third of them go broke. Are you in a position to pay off your first *and* second mortgage from your salary or that of another family member, should you not be able to pay the second back from the company? Are you willing to put the roof over your head at risk on your new venture? Does your partner agree or is this going to be a point of conflict between the two of you?

Your time will be at a premium in the early stages of a new venture and your stress level will be increased as well. You will need understanding and support from your immediate family. Be careful before you add any strain to your relationships. Joint financial risks that are not fully understood will surely increase strain.

If You Use Debt, Understand It

If the only way to finance the venture you are planning is through the use of debt, you need to be educated about how to use it most effectively. First of all, make sure the loan is sufficient to meet *all* of the needs you have budgeted. A start-up loan will likely be secured by all of the business assets so you will be unable to go back and get more. If you run out of capital part way into the project, you will likely hit a dead end. So be very realistic about your pro forma and borrow the total amount you will need to get above breakeven and into profitability. Warning: hold those dollars for use as operating capital and do not be tempted to spend them on desirable but unnecessary items.

You will also need to structure your payback to meet the expected cash flow of the venture. The best possible start-up loan is one that lets you make draws against the available balance for a period of up to a year, paying interest only on the outstanding balance. Once you have drawn the full amount of the loan, you will pay it back over a period of three to five years. One good aspect of this type of financing is that the cash is not in your hands until you actually need it, so you are not paying interest on money you don't need yet. The other is that the principal payback is deferred until such time as your cash flow turns into a positive and you will not be strapped by making these payments. This is a form of start-up debt that could work.

Long-Term Investment Needs Equity

The return on starting a business is over the long term—years and not months. Therefore, the best way to fund a new business venture is with equity capital rather than debt. But there is no reason that all of the equity must be yours. Others gain advantages from investing in your project, and you should understand those advantages so that you may present the concept in a favorable way. The cost to you is that you will be giving up an equity position in your business. The value will be that the loan can be structured so the required start-up money will not have to be paid back until the business is on its feet and profitable. And payback will be directly linked to the available cash flow, making payback even easier.

The most conducive legal entity for having outside investors is a Sub S Corporation. The laws governing such a structure allow you to approach a prescribed number of individuals to offer each a percentage of the company for a cash investment. These laws vary from state to state, but may allow up to 75 individuals; there can be no corporate investment. The current tax laws allow these investors to deduct their share of corporate losses from their personal income tax, which may be a valuable incentive to some potential investors. If you suspect you will have a substantial loss your first year or two, your investors can write off their percentage of ownership from their current income, which means they will reduce their own tax liability. The result is that the net cost of the investment is reduced by that amount.

For example, someone invests $25,000 in your business and gets 10 percent of the outstanding stock. The first year, the company loses $150,000 and this particular stockholder can deduct 10 percent of that loss, or $15,000, from her income tax return. If her tax bracket is 33 percent, she has a reduction on taxes due of a third of $15,000 or $5,000. This means that the $25,000 investment now only cost her a net of $20,000, yet she is still due a payback of $25,000 plus interest. Future losses would have the same benefit. Future profits would be taxable to her, whether or not the profit was distributed in cash to her; on the other hand, if there is no distribution, she has a chance to grow the value of her collateral.

Finding Potential Investors

Typically, a new entrepreneur looks to family and friends to borrow money for the new venture. Even if the investors understand that these loans are high risk and they may have to wait for pay back, they may still be interested in investing in your venture. The reality is that, whether described as a loan or an investment, all of the capital is at risk in any start-up business because a substantial number of businesses do not grow into thriving enterprises. The question for you is, are you comfortable trying to make a "strictly business" deal with people you are close to, or will you feel very guilty if their money is lost? Certainly, you never want to risk the money of anyone who cannot afford it. But however you describe the money, as a loan or an investment, the only return will come from the ultimate success of the venture.

Another way to go is to find outside investors who are at arm's length from you personally. There are a number of ways you must prepare before you even begin to determine who may be good candidates and how you will approach them. The only businesses that are attractive to investors are those that will eventually make a high return on their ongoing operations. The more speculative a company is, the higher the reward if it is successful and the more interesting an opportunity for an outsider. And normally, these are the companies that need the highest level of capitalization, not just for start-up expense, but as operating capital until products are developed or markets are reached. Breakeven may be anywhere from two to five years down the road.

To determine your company's eligibility as an attractive investment, you must create a longer term pro forma profit and loss statement than the average start-up needs. You should try to do at least quarterly projections for one or two years beyond breakeven to see the level of profit you will achieve at full sales volume. In some cases, return may be a high percentage of a moderate volume—for example, 10 percent net on sales of $5 million is $500,000 annual profit. Or it may be a moderate percentage on high volume—for example, 3 percent of $20 million for profits of $600,000 annually. Now look at your total capitalization—that is, how much capital you will need to get to an acceptable level of profitability. What amount should be equity and what amount may be debt or loans? At some point, you will be eligible to borrow against assets (particularly if you have start-up equity) and your cash flow may be able to support debt service.

Let's look at a company earning 10 percent return on $5 million in sales. Initial start-up costs were slightly under $500,000, which came from the owner's investment of $100,000 and a loan of the same amount. The shortfall is $300,000. With an eventual return on investment of 100 percent on the equity of $500,000—this is a good candidate for investment. Allocating 30 percent of profits in dividends would give all equity holders a cash return as well as growth of the value of their investment as their equity in the company continued to climb as the business grew. A good deal for an investor, but with a company earning a high rate of return.

Investment amount	$100,000
Equity purchased	15%
Profits from operations	500,000
Percentage of distribution	30%
Amount of distribution	150,000
	(30% of 500,000)
15% of total distribution =	$22,500
Return on $100,000 investment =	22.5%

Exchanging Equity for Capital

The crucial question for you, as an entrepreneur, is how much equity you are willing to give up for a substantial investment. Many entrepreneurs think they can sell off a piece of their venture for a small interest and get substantial funding. This is seldom true. If you sold the $300,000 of investment off in $50,000 increments, you might be able to issue 6–7 percent of the stock for each of those shares, meaning that your total stock sale would be 36–42 percent, leaving you with 58–64 percent. That would leave you in control, which is the way it should be.

A 6 percent owner would receive his percentage of any losses as tax credit. Once profits of $500,000 were reached and 30 percent of that was distributed ($150,000)—the cash return for each $50,000 investor would be $9,000 or 18 percent—an excellent return on their initial money. You cannot guarantee this type of return, but if you think you are creating this kind of profitable venture, why not allow others to share the risk and share the return?

Small investments may be offered to a variety of people whom you already know. A Sub S Corporation limits the number of people you can solicit, so prequalify anyone under consideration before giving them details about your venture. Often good candidates are the professionals in your community such as physicians, dentists, and other members of the medical community. Other business owners may also be interested if your concept is solid and the possibility for return is there.

Prime candidates may be those companies or individuals who will have a direct link to your business, such as potential suppliers or even customers. Who better to understand your idea and its potential? And because they will already be stakeholders, you have solidified your business relationship and given them good reason to be contributing to your success.

What Information Do You Give to Potential Investors?

For the types of investors we have been discussing, a modified version of your business plan is appropriate to give to them. It should include a full and detailed description of the business concept and how you will bring it to reality. Detailed demographics of the potential customer base would be required, as would pro formas. The financial projections you do here should be conservative, showing all of the potential for early loss. They should also cover a longer term than you may have done for your original plan, showing the chance for substantial return once the break-even has been met. You may also want to include a section on "alternative" strategies showing that you have considered a number of different contingencies and have thought through ways of dealing with them. A business plan is your road map to follow, and a loan proposal is a financial document showing projected profit and loss and cash flows. An investment document is a hybrid of the two. You want to be conservative and realistic and at the same time excite your investors about your venture.

Find the Right Accountant

A good accountant who contributes strong professional advice will be one of your most valuable assets, but you will have to find the right individual. Not all professionals have the same level or areas of expertise and not all have the ability to analyze and communicate well. You must do both research and homework to find the accountant that will meet the needs of your company.

There is no doubt that a large firm will provide a wider scope of specialized expertise on a variety of issues, but the cost will be higher, reflecting the extensive resources in these firms. Few start-up or early stage companies are in any position to afford the hourly rate of the more experienced member of a large firm. If you have the need for this service, it is likely that most of your work and your interaction will be with younger, less experienced, and less expensive staff. If you have a basic financial background, this may be sufficient, but if you are like many new business owners and this is your weak spot, you will definitely require more attention.

You might want to start out with the mid-size or even small size firms. You will want to begin by soliciting recommendations from other business owners and your attorney, insurance agent, or banker. A one-person firm may fill your current need but many people who have used one will tell you that there is almost no time for consultation during tax season. However, you will be working with another entrepreneur who will understand your challenges very well. The happy medium for you may be a firm with several partners and a few younger associates as well.

Always interview any professional you have under consideration face-to-face to ask your questions in an informal setting and to judge whether or not the two of you have any personal rapport. You will be working closely together at times and need mutual respect. Fees should be discussed, but other issues should be covered as well. Some of your questions should be:

- Have you worked with many start-up companies?
- Have you looked at our business plan and do you have any suggestions?
- Are you familiar with the industry or type of business we have?
- Does our financing proposal seem feasible? Do our strategies seem reasonable?
- Do you have special relationships with any lenders?
- What is your typical business reporting cycle (how often do you draw statements and conduct reviews)?
- What are your hourly fees? Is there a minimum and do you charge less for the work done by less experienced associates?

You should meet with several candidates in person to see for yourself how you relate to them. These meetings may be valuable as well because you may gain some additional ideas about your business. Any accountant unwilling to have such an interview should not be considered. There is a high level of trust required here and you must be sure you are in the hands of a competent and confident professional.

Most accountants will want to review your statements quarterly if you prepare them in-house, or they will take the records you produce to prepare a quarterly financial statement, which includes a profit and loss statement and a balance sheet. The review should be in person so you can discuss the results, how you have met your goals and targets, and what changes you want to consider. At the end of the third quarter, sometime in the late fall, you will also want to discuss tax planning strategies—namely, whether there are expenses that should be included in the current tax year or others that should be reserved until the beginning of the new year. There is insight, direction, and money saving advice that you can get from your accountant if you use him properly.

Most small businesses have the technology to do their bookkeeping and/or accounting on their PC. This can certainly save you money that you may have spent to have the work done outside, and you will get your reports on a timely basis. Ask your accountant to help you select software, or at least to review your software choice and to help install it and review any changes or upgrades. There are a number of menu-driven, easy-to-learn programs such as Quickbooks and Peachtree as well as the more sophisticated, customized ones. Whatever you choose, keep in mind that your reports are only as accurate as your data input. Computers can't make up for carelessness.

Creating an Accounting System That Has Value

There is a range of ways to do your company's recordkeeping, from a basic one-write system that you do manually to the most complex and sophisticated custom software that is industry specific for restaurants, construction companies, etc. Any or all of these may work for many different types of businesses. The issues to consider are how many transactions you have and how complicated they can be.

Single Entry System

The one-write systems are single entry and often on a cash basis. There is also an accounting service available that has a company deliver copies of its checks and deposits; the service then puts these into profit and loss statement form. Unless yours is a very basic, primarily cash type of business, this report will give you a false reading and you won't know how well or how poorly you are doing in time to correct the mistakes or capitalize on the more effective strategies. If any large customer invoices aren't paid your volume will be off, and if you are unable to pay your bills they won't show up as liabilities. As cash dwindles and fewer bills are being paid, a cash basis statement really gives an increasingly inaccurate reading. You want and need the most timely and responsive information you can get. Set up a system that will provide it.

Double Entry Systems

Basic accounting software such as Peachtree is an easy-to-run and easy-to-understand double entry system. You are protected from misapplying any data in this type of program because you will be able to see your errors in your trial balance. This is the list of credits and debits that you prepare each month that is the basis for your profit and loss statement. If the trial balance is not in balance, you will know that a mistake has been made and you can find the error and correct it so your financial reports work for you.

Your Books Should Give Valuable Data

Once you have found the accountant that you expect to use and you have reviewed how you intend to do your internal record-keeping, you want to make sure that the detail you create in your system gives you the information you need. You accomplish this by customizing your chart of accounts, which was discussed in the first chapter of this book. These are the categories used to give in-depth detail primarily in the areas of income and expense. The income category is under 500 (or 5000) and includes all monies received by the company. Remember that not all these monies are a result of sales. They may also include asset liquidation and investment income. So you will have separate account numbers for any proceeds from loans, or sale of assets, or other revenue that is not primarily as a result of the sale of your goods or services. Here is where you can analyze how your sales are going by showing them in detail.

For example, a shoe store could report all of its sales as 500 Sales—shoes. The problem is that you have absolutely no detail on what types of shoes you are selling and therefore little data on how to manage inventory and what upward and downward trends are happening. A better report might have the following:

500-00	Women's dress—leather
500-01	Women's dress—fabric
500-02	Women's dress—wedding
501-00	Women's casual—leather loafers
501-01	Women's casual—boots
501-02	Women's casual—sandals

You could add categories like these for a long time and perhaps you would want to do so. Whatever details would be of value to you can be broken out in this format. You might want to know sales by category, by customer type (retail, phone order, quantity order, etc.), or geography (state, zip code, etc.). Then as each sale is recorded on the books, it is posted against a specific accounting number, and at the end of each month, you will get your sales results by categories.

The same detail is possible with your expenses. Purchases can be broken down by exact detail, including type and/or specific vendor. When you get your expense report, you will know exactly where the money went and where to look if you want to curb some types of spending.

Setting up these accounts is a job that you should not leave to the discretion of others. You should work on this with the help of your accountant and the inside bookkeeper or controller. Setting up your books is an important step in having the type of information you can use to manage your business and its resources most effectively.

Start Small but Plan Big

All your work to date should have given you the insight that just getting through the starting days of a new business does not make it a success. You must manage carefully and plan to take the company to its next level, where profits begin to flow. Let's look at an example of what new business owners must overcome and how you might prepare and strategize to do so.

Bob and Karen had a long-term plan to open an antique store. For years, they had been successful dealers, finding treasures at garage sales and out-of-the-way places and selling these selected pieces to customers whose taste and interest they had learned to anticipate. Their garage and basement stored much of what they bought and the pieces could not be shown well without a major moving project. A number of items were being saved specifically for the day that this venture would be their full-time occupation.

It was Bob who had the first opportunity to pursue the goal. Offered a corporate buyout at 52, he found himself with a small nest egg and at least ten more years of productive time. Simultaneously, a rental property became available in an area known for upscale shopping and a few other antique shops. The space was bigger than they had first anticipated and the rent a good bit higher, but the opportunity was too good to pass up.

Their business plan had been in place for years, so they pulled it out to update the numbers and weren't really surprised when the overhead expense upped the cost of the entire project. Bob was willing to invest the bulk of his corporate buyout money, and they had anticipated applying for a loan as well. Now it appeared as if they would be $20,000 short. The most logical solution seemed to be taking on a partner instead of a loan, which had been discussed with another dealer that Bob and Karen had worked with on large buyouts. She wanted to be in a permanent shop too, so for her $20,000 investment she received a 25 percent interest and a comparable amount of shop space to market her own inventory.

Rental agreements were signed, workers called in to make interesting and creative changes to the space, and Bob and Karen went out to buy inventory. Every weekend for almost two months they hit the road to find just the right items for their new store. In less than 90 days, they opened the doors of a truly distinctive shop. The first few weeks it seemed as if everyone they knew stopped by to say hello, look around, and wish them luck. Sales were only 60 percent of what they had anticipated, but they felt that this would correct soon.

By the end of month three, the situation didn't look so rosy. Sales had leveled off and were still less than 70 percent of projections; the shop was bulging with inventory, and there was less than $8,000 left in their account. None of the partners had taken a full paycheck yet.

Their worries began to grow on two fronts: How long would this money last to subsidize operations, and how would they finance the advertising and marketing costs they required to move them forward?

This story is repeated time and time again by start-up businesses. Much of the capital raised to start the business is used by opening day and little remains available as needed working capital. Then, when the reality hits that more money is needed, there is no available source.

The primary way to prevent this critical mistake from day one is to realize that growth will be required and reserve resources must be available to fund that growth. You will likely start smaller than you expected. To be profitable, you will have to grow larger than you likely anticipated.

Here are five tips that will assist you in getting your company to the next level:

1. Be *very* conservative about your pro forma—then reduce projected revenue even further. Expectations of vigorous initial sales are the most frequent cause of difficulties for small businesses. Cash flow expectations are seldom met by cash flow realities.

   A new business won't reach a breakeven point for the first year, and if you haven't anticipated this, you won't be prepared with sufficient capital to fund these early months of losses. This cash shortage may prevent your company from moving on to the next level of increased volume that will secure its future success. (In case you missed the message: you'll close up shop, be down the tube, be out of business, etc.)

2. Don't offer partners a fixed percentage for a one-time investment. If you need to find investment for future capital needs, it will inevitably dilute the ownership of early investors. You must be clear about this or risk misunderstandings that can deteriorate into legal battles.

   Your initial business plan should include plans for second and third rounds of growth financing and identify sources (loaned or invested) that may be utilized. This information must be shared with a potential partner; full disclosure is both a legal requirement and a collaborative necessity.

3. Apply for a loan that is larger than your current needs. A nonrevolving line of credit may work best in these circumstances. If you assume you will need $150,000 over the next two years, year one is start-up and year two is the early stage of growth. Make your loan request for a $150,000 non-

revolving loan that you can draw down on an as-needed basis, and by the end of year two, when you've used the full amount, it then terms out in an installment basis.

As you are drawing down, you pay interest on the portion you have used and only when the full amount of the loan has been used will you pay back the principal and interest over the agreed-to payback period.

In your loan documents, you will find a description of the collateral used to secure your loan. Reject the term signifying assets that are "hereby owned or hereafter acquired." You want to keep future assets available for use as collateral should you need to borrow against them.

4. Work to acquire vendor credit in excess of what you may need at the present time. When you open credit with suppliers, request the amount you will need for year two in business, not just the present time. Your volume will grow and if you can use net 30 days income to pay for inventory, that will be a help in your cash flow.

   It is likely that you will have to build up to this level of credit, and one way to accomplish this is to make large purchases from time to time and take care that you pay the invoice in a timely way. You will build lender confidence and the basis of business-credit granting is trust.

5. Don't invest your entire nest egg—keep some to protect yourself personally and to draw on if a good business opportunity comes along. Putting every last dollar you have into a new business venture makes you feel very vulnerable and you may well find yourself there. During the first year of a new business, missed payrolls are possible, and you could delay or damage the potential of your business if your personal needs become critical.

Over the first few years of your new business, you will learn about its operating realities and how to grow it into a success. Plan for it and don't let the unexpected need for capital undermine your progress.

For Bob and Karen, the solutions were painful but necessary. First came an inventory correction sale for their antique store. Then they and their newest partner agreed jointly that a loan was necessary and together they applied for and received a $50,000 line of credit. Now the antique shop finally had enough working capital to do all of the marketing and advertising necessary to grow. By the middle of year two, sales exceeded projections, as did profits.

Take heed from the experience of this business and virtually all new companies: start small, watch your expenses, and plan for success. It's the best way to get there!

CASE STUDY: J.E. Industrial Distributing

1997 start-up—Jack Edmond, founder

At the end of Chapters 3 to 6, you will be introduced to the story of the life of a small business, from start-up through maturity. In his role as a top salesman for a large Ohio distribution company, Jack felt he had reached his peak working for someone else and decided to go out on his own. Sure that most of his customers (and the sales volume) would follow to his new company, he made the transition in full confidence. As you will see, Jack learned a number of difficult small business lessons along the way.

Let the Venture Begin

Let's face the music and dance.

—*Irving Berlin, recorded by Frank Sinatra*

Learning Objectives

Once you have completed this chapter, you will be able to:

✔ Create a bootstrap budget for a start-up business that will conserve capital.

✔ Describe various noncash resources that allow a business to leverage its working capital.

✔ Understand the various banking needs of a business and how to find the most suitable bank and banker.

✔ Determine whether purchase or leasing of new equipment is most advantageous.

✔ Create budgets meant to control costs.

You have prepared for the first day of business by planning a realistic budget and funding it as completely as possible. You have made the effort to learn as much as you can about the operating needs of your prospective company. And you have located and engaged the services of an accountant to assist in setting up your internal recordkeeping and help interpret the results.

If you have neglected any of these steps, now is the time to go back and complete all of the necessary preparations. The work you do in advance will provide greater possibility of success. It is far easier to do research before a situation arises than to respond under pressure to a critical need.

Adopt a Bootstrap Approach

Everyone reacts individually when they walk into a place of business and observe the surroundings. Some customers pay very little attention, and some may be very drawn to a particular look. You may feel that it is important to project an image that will impress anyone who notices such things. But as a business consultant, I automatically total up the costs of such an environment and wonder about how much I, as the consumer, am paying for this and whether or not it is really important to the product or service I am purchasing. It's a lot less expensive to provide good, friendly customer service.

One example is the travel agency I use. Its offices are centrally located, but hardly luxurious. It consists of four desks in a main room, with one small back office for administrative functions and another for the fax and ticket-writing machine. Why should I care how this office looks? I rarely go there. My contact is on the phone and via mail. My concern is their efficiency at getting me what I need and doing so at the competitive price I want. Aren't most travel customers interested in price and service and not in the beauty of the travel office?

Likewise, the esthetics of many business locations are a very subjective issue and the new entrepreneur must make careful and considered decisions about it. A retail operation is certainly more difficult than a service business. The look of your store, the way products are merchandised, and the quality of amenities such as fitting rooms can be far more important in this type of business. You may be making a strong statement to your potential customers by the environment they encounter from the moment they walk into the door. Sparse surroundings may say low-cost products, and luxurious decor says top of the line. Understand what segment of the market you are looking to serve and make sure that your message and your pricing match.

Can you create an interesting look with less money and more personal imprint? Bringing in little touches from home or from secondhand or resale shops can spice up the look and cost less money than the professionally decorated office or shop. Whatever you don't spend setting up the shop is money left to buy inventory, pay bills, and make operations more efficient.

One of the few exceptions to this rule of keeping new business set-ups simple is that of a restaurant. You are selling an experience along with the food, and this begins when the customer walks into the door and looks around. You don't have to spend a million dollars on furniture and decorations, but you will benefit from an interesting and unique ambiance.

Your choices about your environment begin with the selection of location. The better the address, the higher the cost. The more space you have, the higher the cost. The higher the cost, the longer it will take to bring in sufficient revenues to operate profitably. If your location doesn't matter to your customers or clients, be diligent about choosing a space that is utilitarian, yet cost effective. If your business needs a high traffic volume or a specific demographic clientele, the right location may be critical, whatever the cost.

How Much Staff Do You Need?

It is not an unusual situation for a new business owner to wear many, if not all, of the hats in the early days of a business. For many ventures, payroll will always be the highest cost item and keeping it in check from day one is necessary. Do you need an extra salesperson when you open your doors? An assistant may be convenient and sometimes necessary, but do you have enough work to justify one? Unless and until additional employees can produce revenue in line with their cost, they are a luxury you may not want to acquire.

Of course, this will mean more work for you and often the type of work you didn't expect to be doing. But watching your operating capital drain away into payroll costs is not a good alternative. You may be able to use part-time workers or even students to fill in until sales justify hiring a larger staff. What about hiring tempo-rary workers for particularly busy times? You are not obligated to use them any more than is necessary and that makes them a pro-ductive cost.

Another idea for a start-up operation is the use of outside indepen-dent contractors to do some of the work, such as the secretarial, bookkeeping, and janitorial tasks, and to make home deliveries. Be sure you understand the IRS's strict rules about what constitutes an outside contractor. There are a variety of individuals and small companies that are in business primarily to accomplish some of the jobs you need done on a part-time basis, too much for you to accomplish alone but not enough for an additional full-time employee. Why buy a truck and hire a truck driver when you can hire a service to complete the work and do so only when they are needed?

Finding the Right Employees

Not everyone is cut out to work for a small company, particularly one that is in the start-up phase. The early days are very challenging, the work may be exceptionally hard because protocols have not been established, and the rewards may not be as many as one might wish. The only way to find the pioneers who are willing to be a part of this adventure is to be honest with any candidates you interview and/or hire. Let them know you are a new company and you are trying to keep expenditures as low as possible. Also tell them that you do have great hopes and aspirations for the future. The reality is that what it will take to be successful is great effort and a steady eye on the goal. Finding others to join you in this adventure may give you a real advantage in getting there.

Don't sugarcoat the tasks or promise salary or benefits that are beyond your reach to give at this point. You may hope to be able to meet a goal, but be honest that it depends on how quickly your venture makes it to a profitable and positive cash flow. Workers who understand what is required and perhaps are even energized by the opportunity are the perfect persons to help build your new business. And they are less likely to demand more than is reasonable from you during the start-up and early phase of your business life, particularly if you are working as hard and sharing the sacrifice.

Your Own Needs Will Take a Back Seat

As you were creating a start-up budget, you probably gave a good bit of thought to how much money would be available for you to draw as a salary. It is perhaps one of the most complicated questions for any new business owner. You may have assumed that you would draw little for the first few months and then be able to have something that resembled a full salary. It is more than likely that this will not exactly be the case. It will depend on whether you are a direct cost, meaning that you produce revenue by your own service or labor. If this is the case, every sale dollar will have some portion of it that can be directed to you. On the other hand, if you are an administrative or overhead cost, your salary won't be fully funded until breakeven volume has been exceeded.

If you have not reached breakeven and you pay yourself in lieu of paying a vendor, you will eventually be looking for other capital to pay them. In most cases, if you haven't raised enough money in advance, that capital will come from you. In essence, you are borrowing money that will cost interest and paying yourself in taxable dollars. Perhaps you need to cut your personal expenses or draw on savings to pay your way. Then you will be able to take less from the business than you would like until the company can afford you. Sit down with your accountant and determine what plan best meets your own circumstance. Be prepared to moderate your own draw in the start-up phase.

Other Controllable Costs

The company cannot afford to take on any but the most necessary obligations in its infancy. All of the fancy equipment, vehicles, and interesting trips to conventions and shows will have to wait until their costs can be supported by ongoing profits.

And don't make decisions based on the results of just a few good months. Make certain that even in the "soft" months, cash flow will be adequate to pay any of the obligations you are taking on before you start to reward yourself with those things that will make work life easier and more fun.

As to the travel to conventions and meetings, many of these may be very important even to a new business owner. In fact, sometimes it is even more important to you if you still have to learn about new products and services or to meet other industry players. But when cash is still scarce, you must limit yourself to only a few and keep the cost of travel and lodging as low as you can. Go to regional meetings where you can get to your destination by car and stay at the second string hotels instead of the official headquarters. The meetings and education are what you came for. Now is the time to bootstrap every aspect of your business life—the days of rewards are ahead. You need to be in the game long enough to hit a home run. Conserving cash is the best way to stay in play.

When the Revenue Stream Runs Slow

The most frequently reported area of surprise for new business owners is that sales and revenues do not meet their prebusiness expectations. And while in some cases this is reason for concern, for the most part this is the normal experience of a business start-up.

As an entrepreneur starting a new venture you have spent months, if not years, totally immersed in all aspects of your new company. Choosing the location, preparing it, purchasing equipment and perhaps inventory—all have been consuming tasks. Creating an image in print (logo for cards and brochures), advertising, and marketing have fired your creative juices. Clearly you believe in what you have begun, and you are convinced that others will agree or you would not have gone to the work and the trouble of creating the start-up. You know your customers are out there waiting for you to open your doors.

The problem is, they aren't. Most of your potential clients and customers are going about their normal course of business with the professionals, suppliers, and shops they have always done business with. If you have something totally new, they don't know they need what you're offering! Perhaps they know you are preparing to start your business, and they may even intend to patronize you once you do, but until the business is a reality, their commercial life goes on.

The day comes when you open the doors and you wait for the hordes of eager new customers. But only a few show up, and often, after the early novelty wears off, even fewer walk through the doors. You panic and become frustrated. Don't let this happen.

Be realistic in your expectations. Your eventual loyal following may not yet have found you or may intend to utilize you as a regular source, but old habits die hard. Think of your own spending patterns. Don't you go to the same professionals or businesses as much out of habit as intent? Your job is to be there long enough to develop a steady clientele by providing quality and value and something of new interest. Your customer base will develop if you are tenacious. It may be slower than you expect, but over time, you can reach the goals you've established.

The slow growth of revenue is the main reason to conserve cash. The more you drain off, the less time you will have to grow your new venture into prosperity.

Unusual Sources of Cash and Noncash Resources

You are trying to find as much operating capital as you can and conserve all that you have, so you must be as creative as possible in looking for unusual sources. Following are some ways to leverage what you already have.

Free Rent as an Incentive

If you have found a workable location that is slightly off the beaten track and perhaps has been difficult for the owner to rent, you may be able to get a few months of free rent up front as an incentive to sign a long-term lease. Not having that expense early on surely will be of help.

Inventory on Consignment

In order to get their products into your shop or your manufacturing operation, some vendors will put them in on a consignment basis. When you use their material, you are billed for it. The inventory belongs to the vendor. This means that you won't be stuck with any inventory that you don't ever turn into a sale—a real cost savings.

Joint Marketing Programs

Some suppliers offer programs that share marketing costs (including advertising) with businesses that feature and promote the suppliers' products. A number of major brands have these types of co-op funds available. Don't be shy. Ask your vendors if they normally do anything like this. Even if they don't, see if they would consider it. You might be able to create a program that is of value to both of you. Mentioning the name of a specific product and your store in the same marketing material is a win for both of you! After all, your grocery story doesn't advertise all of the brand name products at its own expense.

Barter

If you are conserving cash, what better way to do so than getting goods or services without any cash exchange. One way to accomplish this is to barter your goods or services for those that you need. Be careful that you don't get unnecessary items simply because there is no cash outlay.

You may find a formal barter club that arranges and controls barter deals between members. It charges a fee to join and takes a small commission from each deal. You make available your company's products or services and you earn credits when they are used. Then you "spend" those credits on the goods and services you require. Make sure before joining a club that you can buy things you actually need.

You can barter by identifying companies that could benefit from your services, and you from theirs—and make your own trade.

Vendor Credit

A good source of working capital can be found through the prudent use of vendor credit. This source may take the place of loans and cost you no interest at all.

It is not easy for a start-up company to secure a meaningful amount of vendor credit. Without a track record, most suppliers will want to have payment up-front or ship on a C.O.D. basis. You must learn to negotiate from the beginning and then meet any obligations so that you can later secure the credit you will eventually require.

Why not offer to pay 50 percent in advance and at first, ask for 10 days to pay the balance. You may even offer to send a dated check. Remember, the goal is to win confidence. The next round, you could ask for the balance to be paid in 30 days. Then make absolutely sure you meet that deadline. After a period of time, you may have up to a certain dollar limit on a net 30 day basis. That's progress.

Evening out cash flow through vendor credit is a good way to finance the growth you will need and your supplier wants as well. As your company gets larger and stronger, your suppliers get a bigger customer. Remember, they want you to succeed.

Customer Deposits

If you have customers that have placed customized or particularly large orders or have arranged long-term contracts with your business, one way to finance the overhead required to fulfill the orders is to ask for a substantial payment in advance. In fact, any time a customer orders a very specialized product, you should insist on a deposit that assures you won't get stuck with goods for their order that you can't move elsewhere.

However, you must remember that all cash received for a specific piece of business should be used to complete only that order or contract. Using new money to pay old debt is a sign of trouble, and before long you will find yourself unable to finish current work unless the next cash customer comes along. Unfinished work is a liability because your customer won't accept partially completed products or jobs. You would have to pay back the deposit money you received—and your reputation would be damaged. So while deposits may be a good source of operating capital, they should be used with care.

Open Your Account at the Right Bank

Many new business owners give little thought about developing a banking relationship and just open their new business account at the closest bank. This may be a real mistake. Your banker is one of your most important vendors, yet you are likely to have taken far greater care in choosing most of your other vendors. The product supplied by your bank is not only money but a variety of other financial services, and if you have chosen well, you also may receive valuable technical assistance.

Your first decision is whether to use the branch of a large bank or find a smaller community bank. There are far fewer choices now than there were ten years ago. As a result of all of the mergers, many cities have only two or three major players; many of the smaller or mid-size banks have been gobbled up or consolidated. For the most part, the mid-size bank is a relic of the past. Your decision now will likely be between a small or a large banking institution. Base your decision on the types of services that you will require as your company grows.

If, over the next few years, you think that you will need some sophisticated banking services such as lock-box service (where your checks are sent directly to the bank), estate or trust management, or perhaps international banking such as letters of credit to finance some importing, you may want to look to a larger institution. They will have entire departments that specialize in these areas, as well as others. For example, if you expect to have excess cash in your account on a short-term basis and want to have it regularly moved between your regular account and an interest bearing account, you may be beyond the small bank's ability.

Also consider how you normally collect and deposit money. If you handle a lot of cash and need to make frequent deposits, the location of a branch is important to you from a convenience and safety standpoint. You could use a bonded truck service for this, but that would add cost, and you are trying to be cost efficient.

And finally, you will want to consider what types of loans your company will require as it begins to grow and needs more working capital. All banks can write term loans and lines of credit that are straightforward. But perhaps you will be looking for a Small Business Administration guarantee. Newer companies often do because this guarantee supplements their collateral and allows the bank to be more flexible. Make sure the bank you have chosen will write an SBA guaranteed loan. All can but not all want to because of the added paperwork.

Perhaps you will need more complicated types of lending. For example, you may require special contract financing where the loan is collateralized by an order and retired as the work is complete. In that case, you may be out of the league of a small bank. A loan that requires a good bit of monitoring requires a bank that has sufficient personnel to do this.

You are building for the long-term financial stability of your company. Take the time to make the best choice of banks and bankers. Stop by one or more institutions that you are considering and meet the managers. Although bank personnel moves around, managers are often at a location for a long stay. Introduce yourself and explain that you are a new business owner in the area. Judge his or her interest in who you are and what you are doing. Does the manager ask questions and seem knowledgeable about your new venture? Do the two of you seem to relate well? After all, your banker is the one who will be dealing with you and making some decisions with regard to some early needs you may have. That manager may not be your commercial lender, but you will need his or her help and recommendation on day-to-day banking issues.

Are you aware that not all of your funds are available as soon as they are deposited? It may take 24 to 72 hours before they are considered collected funds. Your bank may refuse to clear any checks that have been written against uncollected funds. Once you have established a track record at the bank, your manager may be willing to sign off on such clearances. Having a relationship with your manager can aid in having checks cashed, cashier or treasury checks drawn for you, wire transfers completed, and, occasionally, bank fees waived. Making the most effective use of your time and money makes good sense, and finding and cultivating the best bank and banker is a part of that.

If you know you want to deal with a larger banking institution that has multiple branches, but you aren't sure about the local manager, feel free to visit some of the other branches too. You can have both the convenience of transacting in the closest location yet who work with a manager who seems more in tune to your needs by making his or her branch the one that houses your account.

You should understand, though, that banks do not make money from handling your business checking account. For the most part, that is a cost to them in recordkeeping and the administration of paying checks drawn. Some banks even create a cost analysis of your spending along with your regular statement, and charge fees to recover costs of the extra report. What a bank does make money on is any services it provides for fees, and certainly from the interest it charges on loans. Knowing how the bank makes money helps you conserve yours and helps you shape a business relationship where the bank can provide services you need, but only when you request them as your needs change.

Leasing or Buying Equipment?

The first loans you may be thinking about may be for the purpose of purchasing new equipment or new vehicles. These loans are not as difficult to find as others because they are well secured on the asset you are buying. At this point, should you be buying any assets or should you be leasing them? There are advantages both ways. Your banker may actually be a resource on both ends because many banks have separate leasing departments.

The major benefit of leasing at this point in time may be the lower up-front cost when you are trying to conserve cash. A purchase may require up to 20 percent of the cost as a down payment, while a lease may cost only a security deposit. This allows you to hold on to your current cash as operating capital, which is what you want at this stage of your business.

Another benefit is that leasing may be easier for a new company with little or no track record. The title to the equipment or vehicle remains in the hands of the leasing company. Many of these companies work closely with the equipment manufacturers so there are incentives and buy back arrangements that lower your risk even more. Car companies have long had their own leasing businesses because it is a profit center both ways: they move more cars and they make money from the leases.

Another advantage in a lease is the possibility of turning back the vehicle or equipment at the end of the contract time (or sooner) and replacing it with a new model. There are times when the use of the equipment is more desirable than the ownership because you want periodic upgrades without the hassle of selling the existing equipment. While there is an overall cost to this benefit but for many new businesses, it is worthwhile for the convenience.

There are tax advantages to leasing over buying. Having a loan will allow you to deduct only the interest portion of the loan. In most operating leases, all of the costs of your payments are fully deductible. This becomes more important as you have taxable income that you want to shelter.

In the early days of your company, your balance sheet will be a bit weak, as you have not yet started to acquire any real assets. A loan used to purchase equipment or vehicles will show up on your balance sheet as a liability, and you will be fully depreciating the value of the asset, which will affect your profit and loss statement. While your lease payment is an expense that will appear on your profit and loss statement, the additional depreciation cost will not, thereby lowering the effect on your profitability. If you are making good profits, you would want the noncash expense (depreciation) to help lower taxes.

Leasing contracts are not seen as primary lending, but as a secondary source of funds, and will not show up as a loan. Therefore, you will still be eligible for primary loan funds as a source of working capital. Most lending institutions limit the amount of loan funds you can access based on your assets and cash flow. You want to keep as much credit available as you can to get over soft spots and to take advantage of opportunities.

You should consider that there are drawbacks to not owning equipment outright, aside from the fact that the overall cost is higher. Because you are not the owner, any changes or modifications will require the permission of the lessor. If your upgrades have added to the equipment's value, the lessor will acquire the benefit of that value, not your company. You will, however, benefit from the use of improved equipment. Discuss leasing versus buying with your accountant.

Control Costs by Tracking Them

When you were first writing your business plan, you probably were very busy learning how to create a pro forma and trying to project numbers that would show you the reality of your venture in real dollars and cents. Once you opened the doors, you inevitably had some surprises. Some were good, I hope. Perhaps some items didn't cost as much as you had anticipated. And I know some were not quite so positive. There were some line items that grossly exceeded your estimations—utilities perhaps, or the cost of insurance. And perhaps you came across some expenses you didn't expect at all, such as building repairs or freight costs. You can never find out the real costs of operating a business until you are operating a real business.

How do you keep costs under control so that they don't exceed the amount you have set aside to cover them? Simple in principle, yet sometimes difficult in practice—set a budget and stick to it!

Begin by comparing projections to actual expenses. Hopefully the overall dollar expenditure hasn't been exceeded, even if the categories may have distinctly different numbers in them.

The next step is to reallocate your dollars according to:

- Current actual costs
- Expected near-future needs

Take each and every line item and analyze it fully. Have you been overspending? Have you not spent enough on items such as marketing or education? What would be a dollar goal to spend (or perhaps a percentage of gross sales)? Recalculate your entire pro forma into a line item budget format and create it on a month-by-month and quarterly basis. Make sure you account for any annual expense such as fees and insurance renewals.

Now, at the end of each month, cost your profit and loss statement on a budgeted and actual basis so that you can judge how you've done compared to how you've budgeted. Because some costs may lag or accelerate, you may want to wait until the end of each quarter to institute any changes. Be sure before you make any changes that what you are looking at isn't just a one-time event.

Track your inventory in this process as well. It is expensed under cost of goods sold. Track your actual usage closely to make sure your cost amount is being met. If you are using more inventory than you anticipated, you must take steps to correct it immediately.

Your first days in business are very critical. They set the stage for many years to come. You are still inside the learning curve, with much of the hands-on experience unknown to you. Learn to keep a tight lid on your costs in the beginning. Conserve your capital so you can survive long term and give yourself some time to learn all the tricks of the trade. Your goal is long-term success. You don't get there overnight.

CASE STUDY

J. E. Industrial Distributing Company was started in 1977 by Jack Edmond, the top salesperson of another of Ohio's largest distribution companies. Jack had grown to a 1976 personal sales volume in excess of $5 million and he believed that most of his customers would follow him and purchase from his new company. The gross profit margin he had established with his original employer was 23 percent with a direct cost of 77 percent of goods, based on prices delivered to their warehouse. All sales people set their own margins, which were the basis of their compensation. Jack's was the highest in the company. Jack based his original start-up budgets and pro forma statement on these assumptions. His business plan and loan request for $400,000 included the following financial estimates:

Start-Up Budget

Inventory	$600,000[1]
Leasehold improvements	35,000[2]
Trucks (2)	25,000[3]
Shelving	10,000
Office equipment	20,000
Working capital	200,000[4]
Total required	$890,000

Sources of Capital

Owner's investment	$150,000
Vendor credit	140,000
Bank loan	600,000
Total required	$890,000

[1] Based on $400,000 month in volume—this was 45 days inventory

[2] Converting a portion of the warehouse into offices

[3] Two used step vans for delivery

[4] Expected overhead for first 90 days

His first year pro forma projected the following:

Quarter:	1	2	3	4	
Sales income	$1,000,000	$1,000,000	$1,200,000	$1,200,000	
Cost of sales	770,000	770,000	924,000	924,000	77%
Gross profit	230,000	230,000	286,000	286,000	23%
General and administrative expense:					
Rent	12,000	12,000	12,000	12,000	
Salaries[5]	26,700	26,700	26,700	26,700	
Office expense	15,000	15,000	15,000	15,000	
Telephone	10,500	10,500	10,500	10,500	
Utilities	1,500	1,500	1,500	1,500	
Travel/ entertainment	15,000	15,000	15,000	15,000	
Marketing	4,500	4,500	4,500	4,500	
Interest[6]	18,000	18,000	18,000	18,000	
Owner's draw	21,000	21,000	21,000	21,000	
Total cost	124,200	124,200	124,200	124,200	12%
Profit (before tax)	$ 105,800	$ 105,800	$ 161,800	$ 161,800	

Jack's estimates turned out to be overly optimistic, creating some early-stage difficulties for the new company.

Discussion Questions

1. How should start-ups base their sales and revenues? How conservative or risky should those projections be?

2. Are historical numbers a realistic baseline figure? Why or why not?

3. Should profit margins be projected higher or lower than anticipated to adequately prepare for actual results?

4. How much working capital is required to provide a margin of safety?

---

[5] Staff included receptionist, bookkeeper, warehouse worker, truck driver, and second salesperson at a $3,000/month draw

[6] Twelve percent on 600,000

The Art of Business

Some see private enterprise as a predatory target to be shot, others as a cow to be milked, but few are those who see it as a sturdy horse pulling the wagon.

—Winston Churchill

Learning Objectives

Once you have completed this chapter, you will be able to:

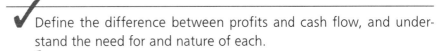

✔ Define the difference between profits and cash flow, and understand the need for and nature of each.

✔ Create a cost effective marketing plan with consideration to the actual value of each new customer.

✔ Determine the hidden value of a product/service that enhances its profitability.

✔ Analyze the pricing strategies of a product and determine the price point that maximizes margins as well as volume.

✔ Develop credit and collection policies that are effective.

✔ Understand how to use basic financial ratios.

Your doors have been open for a while and you have begun to develop a customer base. Now the reality of your business operation is coming into focus. Perhaps you are seeing sales come on line a bit slower than you planned or hoped. But be assured that as long as you are seeing steady progress in revenue growth, you are on the right track. You are learning about your customers' preferences and you now have identified trends in costs as well as the effect of your pricing. You are learning where your existing customers see value and at what price point they begin to show some resistance. In short, you are learning under real conditions how to operate your business effectively: when to make some mid-course corrections and when to stand pat. You should never be afraid to make changes along the way. Responding to the market is the real key to greater success.

Cash Flow versus Profits—The Critical Difference

In the first chapter, we described the elements of a profit and loss statement, the document that shows you if you are making any money from the sale of your products or services. A cash flow statement shows you how real dollars flow in and out of your company on a weekly or monthly basis and whether you're making a profit. These two are not the same. It is possible to make a profit and still not have sufficient cash flow. On the other hand, it is equally possible to be losing money and have enough cash flow to cover your expenses for a while. Consider the airline industry. All airline tickets are paid for prior to use, either in cash or by credit card. In some cases, due to the pricing of advance ticket purchases, money is received long before any service is performed. This is cash inflow and the outflow happens only after the travel has actually taken place, when wages are due, fuel and other supplies must be paid for, or leases and loans are due. An airline can easily find itself deep in a hole before it begins to feel any real capital pains. This is the fate that has befallen most of the new start-up airlines. They burn up capital trying to get passenger loads up, and eventually even the good cash flow can't make up for ongoing losses because income is less than outgo.

The reason that you must have capital with a long-term payback to fund early losses is that any return of that investment will come back slowly over a period of time in the form of profits. Once you are in the black (making a profit), you will still need working capital to fund any growth that you have. For most businesses, cash lags behind the sales, and funding the expense of growth can cause a very serious cash crunch.

The sooner in the life of your business you begin to experience this growth, the tougher it may be to fund it because until you have secured sufficient vendor credit to support increased purchases or bank loans to pay payroll and overhead, you will need capital to fuel the growth.

Let's look at an example of a company in year two, now making a profit but growing at the rate of 20 percent for the year. Look at how its cash gets strangled. We'll assume it has yet to get any loans, so there is no debt service. Sales at the beginning of the year were at $50,000 per quarter, and by the fourth quarter they were at $70,000, with a profit of 6 percent of gross. The company's starting cash was only what was collected from the previous period and not spent, which was a shade more than $10,000. Sales were often on credit and took 45 days to turn into cash, so only two thirds of sales, including collections from previous months' sales, were collected in the current month.

What you can see from this chart is that the company is both growing and profitable, but the cash is short and the situation is getting more difficult as time goes on. The value of the revenue growth is there in the form of accounts receivable, which is an asset showing on the balance sheet, so the worth of the business is going up even as the operating problems are becoming increasingly more difficult to manage. If left uncorrected, meaning no additional capital is infused, these problems can stop any further growth and even jeopardize the business itself.

	Quarter 1	Quarter 2	Quarter 3	Quarter 4
Sales income	$50,000	$55,000	$65,000	$70,000
Direct exp (60%)	30,000	33,000	39,000	42,000
Gross profit (40%)	20,000	22,000	26,000	28,000
Overhead	17,000	18,700	22,100	23,800
Net before taxes	$ 3,000	$ 3,300	$ 3,900	$ 4,200
Starting cash	$10,000	$ (4,000)	$(16,700)	$(32,800)
+ Collections	33,000	39,000	45,000	55,000
Total available	43,000	35,000	28,300	22,200
Less direct	30,000	33,000	39,000	28,000
Less overhead	17,000	18,700	22,100	23,800
Less debt	0	0	0	0
Ending cash	$(4,000)	$(16,700)	$(32,800)	$(29,800)

How to Smooth Out Cash Flow

In cases where there is no source at all for additional outside capital, the best way to handle the situation is to extend or reverse the timing of money coming in and going out. A very serious collections program (which will be discussed more fully later in this chapter) is the first part of this program, as is slowing down the payment of bills that you owe. You can extend your outgoing payments by 10 days or so without alarming most of your vendors and the extra time in the cash cycle, along with faster collections, will substantially ease the cash flow burden.

This is also probably the time for you to begin to approach your bank with a request for a working capital loan. Profits are there and collateral is growing, so once this phase has slowed, cash flow will catch up and should be sufficient to service any debt. A line of credit that you draw on when needed and pay back as your money is collected may work well at this point. You also may want to be able to accept credit cards for payments, as this will speed cash collections. The wait for payment from the credit card company is from 24 to 48 hours normally. It may be difficult for a new business to secure a merchant account but it is worth trying. Your bank may be a good resource and there are a number of private transaction companies. Look into it: people who may otherwise take 30 days to pay you may be willing to "put it on plastic." The next chapter, on growth, will discuss this step more fully. You want to solidify your financial operating strategy.

Analyze the Value of Your Marketing Program

There are a number of overhead costs that a business assumes without fully understanding their value or how to allocate the most effective amount of capital resource. Marketing is often one of these costs. Some new businesses spend substantial money on a fairly broad based approach. When they see few results, they give up the entire program. Others see it as a luxury they can't afford and spend virtually no money at all on it. Both behaviors are counterproductive.

Marketing is a necessity. It is a long-term investment in your business that will generate the interest in your company that will turn into sales down the road. Basically the difference between marketing and sales is that the former creates the awareness and the latter converts awareness into financial transactions. You won't have customers if no one knows where you are and what you offer. On the other hand, knowing of your existence and even having some serious interest in your company won't bring you actual dollars until you make a sale.

You Must Learn the Value of Each New Customer

How much should you spend to attract a potential customer? This is a critical question for you to answer before you set up your marketing budget. Your goal should be to set aside an amount sufficient to make an impact, yet economical enough to be able to sustain over the long haul. Overspending, as many new companies do, will only cause you to cut back drastically later, just when the marketing is doing its job.

Remember, you are creating opportunities, so you want to determine what the direct economic benefit is to you in terms of revenue and gross profit per customer. In essence, you are looking to find what an average customer brings into the doors of your company. Then you can decide how much to spend to develop a new customer.

Begin by dividing your total sales by the number of customers you currently are serving. Of course, you may have some superstars who spend a good bit of money with you, as well as a few whose numbers are fairly small. But as you cannot predict what type of spender a new customer may be, you want to use the average as a benchmark.

Let's say, for example, that your current sales are $300,000 and you are serving a client base of 25. This means your average income is $12,000 of revenue per customer. If your gross margin is 40 percent, then you are making an operating profit on each of $4,800. Now you can allocate a percentage to your marketing program. Depending on whether or not your other overhead costs are in line, perhaps 5 percent of your total overhead cost can be dedicated to marketing expense. Assume you want to grow at a rate of 50 percent—that is, find 12 new customers providing fresh gross profits of $57,600 ($4,800 × 12) per year. So you will allocate 5 percent of $57,600, or $2,880, for your new customers, plus $6,000 for the maintenance of your existing customer base. You must continue to spend to keep your name in front of your current client base to keep them interested and coming back. Setting an approximate budget of $9,000 a year on $300,000 of revenue is very reasonable. It is 3 percent of your gross sale dollar.

Next, make sure you get the biggest bang for your buck. Even if marketing isn't your special skill, you should realize that spending any money without careful consideration isn't wise. One of the most critical aspects in a well-conceived marketing plan is knowing who is the most likely candidate to become a new customer. Of course, you will learn a lot from your current customer base. If you are currently selling to businesses, you can determine:

- Size of company—how many employees?
- Location—local, national, or international?
- Industry—wholesale or retail?

If you are selling to individual consumers, you want to know:

- General demographics—age, sex, and education
- Geographic area
- Other general interests

Consumers vote with their dollars, and the ones who have chosen to do business with you have sent you a message. Finding more of the same types is an astute way to go. Reach more of these people by advertising in publications they are likely to read or by sending direct mail to a specific demographic group or geographic location. Tailor each message to a specific audience. Let them know who you are, what exactly you do, and what benefits there are in doing business with you.

Much of the marketing background data gathering can be done by you or someone within your organization. The idea is to be cost effective. There are great firms that you can hire to do a terrific job at marketing communication but the question is, Do you have the money? Down the road when you can afford it, that may be the most cost effective way to go because your time has great value as well. But for now, yours is a new company and still conserving cash.

On the other hand, you absolutely cannot afford to neglect his aspect of your business. You won't grow if potential customers aren't aware that you're there. Keep your name and image in front of the public. If you absolutely can't do this for yourself, hire someone—but do it!

Keep Your Message Consistent

The other aspect to an effective marketing strategy is to keep your look and your message clear and strong. You want people to remember you, and that will happen if they see and hear something distinctive on a regular basis. That's why companies have slogans. "It's the peanutiest." "We bring good things to life." If you create too many clever looks or stories, each one may get some attention, but they won't have the cumulative effect you are seeking. Think of all the commercial logos or jingles you recognize easily because you have seen or heard the same thing a number of different times over a long period. That's what you want for your strategy: something memorable.

Added Value—Added Profits

There were a number of pizza chains that were fairly successful over the years but a real explosion came when Domino's opened up and guaranteed to deliver a hot pizza in 30 minutes or less. Even though that guarantee has been withdrawn for safety reasons, the fast-delivery pizza business has grown tremendously, and Domino's led the way. Same old business, new twist.

Consider this strategy in light of your own business. Are you doing the same thing, selling the same products in the same way as others? What is it that differentiates you from your competition? Are you able to put a new twist on an old concept?

There is great value in giving your client or customer something additional that provides an incentive for choosing your business over another, on a basis other than price. If people seek you out for a special reason, they will be prepared to pay a bit more; that is where you want your business to be positioned. Some ideas:

- Free delivery—as busy as most people are, any convenience has value.

- More convenient store hours—with couples working long hours, early morning or later evening hours are appreciated. How about a day care center or 24-hour telephone or Web site service?
- Sourcing of hard to find products—special sizes or out of production items still in demand but no longer carried by mass merchandisers.
- Orders by fax or e-mail—making it easy to do business with you.

There are a number of ways you can exceed the needs of your own customers, and in return, you will be able to add a percentage to your pricing and much of that will go directly to your bottom line. After all, 3 percent of $500,000 in volume is $15,000—most of that will be your profit. Too many new business owners are more concerned by the top line, the gross sales, than they are by the bottom line or the profit. That's the money you keep—that's what you're in business for. Learn to compete on value, not price.

Set Prices at Profitable Levels

There are a number of different elements involved in pricing your products or services—things you must take into consideration when deciding how much of a markup you will add. One is internal—the actual cost, and the other is external—the current market sensitivity to pricing.

You must start by knowing exactly what it costs you to produce your item, purchase your product for resale, or provide your service to your client. Then you must fully consider what the current market price is for that product or service at your quality. If you are pricing too high, you will likely see customer resistance. But if you are pricing too low, chances are you are missing out on the profits you require. The challenge is to generate sufficient business at a price point that makes sense. You may need to try out a few pricing strategies over the first months of operation in order to find out what works for you. One way to do this is to run a grand-opening sale, first setting your prices where you would like them to be but offering a discount for a short period. As you allow your prices to go back to their desired point, you can find out how much effect this has on your volume. Don't make discount sales a regular occurrence though. There are some companies that have made their customer base dependent on sales and they see little or no activity during nonsale times.

Know Your Direct Costs

The cost of material in a manufacturing operation or of finished goods in a wholesale or retail business are the first part of direct costs—those directly involved in each sale. These are also known as variable costs because they vary according to the volume of goods being sold. The more you sell, the directly higher the cost.

You must know exactly the dollar amount of the material you have in the goods you sell, and you must include a number of other costs that are involved in acquiring the material. One is the incoming freight if you are the one who pays for it. Even though the payment of inbound freight may be expensed as an administrative cost, you must still break it out and consider how much it adds to each item.

The most difficult added cost to figure is that of shrinkage—the cost of any material or products that will not be used or be sold. In the case of material for manufacturing, the causes for this adjustment may be that some material is wasted during the manufacturing process, rejected for quality flaws or bought in excess and not used at all. It would not be unusual to see an add-on of 8–10 percent for this factor. In the area of resale of finished products, the primary scenario is inventory that moves slowly or not at all. You may dispose of this inventory by selling it off at a deep discount (perhaps cost or below) or liquidating the goods substantially below cost to a broker. Again, you may have up to 10 percent of

CHAPTER 4 / THE ART OF BUSINESS

your total purchases in this category. You must turn over your inventory because the older it gets, the less valuable it is.

If you don't consider the cost of inventory loss, then you may believe you are close to or making a profit but finding yourself in a growing cash crunch. Your inventory will be building with unsold and unused merchandise, and when you eventually write it down, you will take the hit all at once against your bottom line. Better to account for it in your pricing and mark up to cover the cost.

The other component of direct costs is any labor directly related to the production or sale of goods or the labor involved in providing a service. When you price, you must also consider all of the "excess" costs involved in labor, such as benefits (paid vacation, insurance, etc.), and any taxes. Typically, the add-on cost of benefits to any labor costs is 28–30 percent. Therefore, $100 of direct labor will actually cost you $130.

If you do not establish your pricing on the entire direct cost of your goods or services, you will find that your gross margin is not sufficient to cover overhead and you will be netting only a marginal profit or losing money. And, of course, cash will be tight.

Establishing Profit Markup

The other costs you will cover from your gross profit will be those that are indirect or fixed. That means that they stay about the same regardless of the volume of business that you have. In order to find the percentage of gross profit you must have, you will need to determine what you expect to reach as a volume goal in the start-up phase of the company. For example, you may have determined that the annual fixed overhead (rent, utilities, office staff and officers' wages, sales and marketing expense, etc.) is $150,000. You expect that sales will reach $600,000 by the end of the year. Your overhead percentage is 25 percent of gross sales, so in order to make a profit, your direct costs must be marked up by approximately 30 percent. Your gross profit (30 percent of $600,000) would be $180,000—sufficient to cover expenses and show a profit. Always add a bit extra in your prices so you can offer discounts or incentives without seriously damaging your bottom line.

Now, Account for the Competitive Factor

How much latitude you have in your pricing depends greatly on what type of business you are in, how unique your product or service is, whether you sell brand name items that can be easily price compared, and how much direct competition you have. Find out what the range is for the same or similar products or services in your area (that is, the market that you serve, which may be regional or national). Then determine where you fit in the perceived-value scale. Is your shop more convenient? Do you offer extra service? Do you have a higher level of expertise? Price yourself equivalent to your full value.

Take for example the restaurant business. It is often the case that two different restaurants within a few miles of each other charge vastly different prices for the same food. A steak may be $12.95 at one and $19.95 at the other. The difference *may* be in the cut and quality of the meat, but it is also likely to be in the surroundings and the service. One restaurant may offer fine dining, and the other may be seen as a family restaurant; they will charge accordingly.

You can always readjust your prices if you have gone a bit high, but it is far more difficult to raise prices once they have been set. If you find that you are not in a comfortable profit range, then you must review your operation. Can you change the product mix for higher markups or reduce your overhead to lower costs? Over the long haul, setting prices too low will destroy your business operation.

The Impact of Price Cuts

If you have learned your breakeven numbers well, you will realize that the higher your volume gets above that point, the less of an impact overhead has. Therefore, rapid growth may seem a desirable goal. But what if that growth comes at the cost of lower prices? Can you really create enough demand by reducing your selling price to overcome the drop in gross profit margins?

You might be very surprised to see how much of a volume increase you require in order to make up for lower prices and the accompanying lower profit margins. For example:

Your product has a current selling price of $100. The direct cost is $65. You sell 150 items each month. Your current gross profit margin is as follows:

150 units @ $100	=	$15,000
direct cost of $65/unit	=	9,750 or 65%
gross profit	=	5,250 or 35%

A price decrease of 10 percent would lower each unit price to $90. Your gross profit would be:

150 units @ $90	=	$13,500
direct cost of $65/unit	=	9,750 or 72%
gross profit	=	3,750 or 28%

It would require a 40 percent increase in sales to produce the same gross profit dollars that you had before the price cut—and you know what a task it is to grow at that rate.

210 units @ $90	=	$18,900
direct cost of $65/unit	=	13,650 or 72%
gross profit	=	5,250 or 28%

Not only is this a very substantial growth rate, but also the reality is that your overhead is bound to go up a bit just to handle this increase in volume. You will be handling substantially more product and paperwork and will require support for sales. So while you have just gotten back to the gross profit dollars you had in the beginning, you will not be seeing anywhere near the net profit you had. Is it worth it? Unless you are geared up to be a high volume/low markup player, it is not. Be careful before choosing the price-lowering strategy: once you have headed in that direction, it is almost impossible to change course.

The Effect of Raising Prices

The other side of the coin of lowering prices is instituting a price increase. Perhaps you will find that some of your customers are very price sensitive and may go elsewhere at even the slightest increase. The concern about this possibility is what stops most business owners from attempting to raise prices, even when their costs go up. But you may be surprised to look at the effect of raising prices and to realize how much of a risk you may be able to take.

For example, start with the same former unit price of $100, sale of 150 units, and direct cost of $65. As indicated earlier:

150 units @ $100	=	$15,000
direct cost of $65/unit	=	9,750 or 65%
gross profit	=	5,250 or 35%

With a price *increase* of 10 percent and a sales drop of 10, you will find the following:

```
135 units @ $110          =    $14,850
direct cost of $65/unit   =     8,775 or 59%
gross profit              =     6,075 or 41%
```

So you see, even with a 10 percent drop in sales, your gross profit dollars are up by 15 percent! Perhaps the way to go is higher prices and less volume because just as higher gross sales revenue will increase overhead, less volume will result in less paperwork and lower handling costs, resulting in higher net profits. Look closely at this strategy; it is not the top line that matters; it is the *bottom line.*

Pricing Makes a Statement

Sales may be influenced by the phenomenon of snob appeal—the higher the price, the more the perceived value. If you have started up your business in a high rent district and added all the bells and whistles to the shop or office, high prices are likely expected by people who choose to come through your door. If you have chosen the opposite location and decor, you are less likely to be able to sustain any higher-than-normal markups. The mid-range strategy is the safest to attract the most new customers. Your prices should more than cover all of your costs (you need to monitor these constantly), yet remain in the competitive ball park.

If you are in the early stages of operation and your volume has not reached the levels that you had hoped for and expected, don't automatically believe that your pricing is the culprit. Once you understand the effect of price cuts, you can make knowledgeable decisions about using them.

Getting Paid on Time

Making a profit is your goal, but if you don't collect your money in a timely fashion, your cash flow won't benefit from your hard work. The only way to correct any deficiencies in this area is to establish formal credit and collection policies and stick to them. The time to begin this activity is at the point of sale. Know who the customers are and their prior credit with the company. Document your transactions. You will thus minimize your problems.

Grant Credit Carefully

No doubt, credit has become a way of life in this culture. Few people bother to carry much cash and pay for all of their purchases by check, credit card, or debit card. If you are selling to individual consumers, you will want to accept both credit and debit cards. There is a cost to this service—a percentage of each sale, but it is well worth it for the positive effect on your cash flow. The average sale on credit is higher than that in cash and you see your money very quickly. But remember, credit card processing companies differ as to fees charged. Also, turnaround time (the time it takes the money to be deposited in your account) may be as short as 24 hours or as long as 72 hours. Shop around; ask your bank or ask private transactors about rates and terms. If your credit card volume is likely to be high, negotiate a good deal for yourself based on volume.

Business-to-business credit is a different story altogether. If you grant credit to a company, there is a good chance that you will do so on your own receivables. You are at risk until the invoice is paid, so be cautious. Of course you want to make the deal, but to make it and never get paid won't keep you in business for very long.

Establish a credit procedure—use a credit application and make sure it is filled out completely and then signed by the company looking for an open account. This demands that your customer accepts responsibility, and on some applications the signer is accepting personal as well as corporate lability. Whether or not to demand a personal guarantee in your business is a judgment call—you don't want to offend, but you do want to protect yourself.

Check References

Ask for a bank reference as well as three credit references and then make sure to call the references to check. You will be getting their best vendors but you may learn something by calling and asking. Ask how long the account has been open and what the high credit has been. You may find out that others have limited their exposure and you will want to follow suit.

Based on the information you have secured, you'll want to set an opening limit for credit. You want your customers to be able to get what they need (and what you hope to sell them), but you want to be prudent as well. Starting a bit low and then offering a chance to increase may be the way to go. You also may want to ask for a deposit upfront; that will at least cover your out-of-pocket expenses. Be creative, be flexible, but most important, be prudent. Don't take any greater risk than you have to.

Ask Important Questions

Don't be afraid to ask very specific questions of new customers about how they normally pay their bills. In fact, having a live person assure you that you will be paid in 30 or 45 days will allow you to go back to that same person and remind him or her of the promise. And don't hesitate to call a large corporation to investigate its payment procedures. Some of the worst payment terms are used by the large companies because they know they can usually get away with it and they have set up systems that are so cumbersome that invoices always process slowly. But you can often find out what you are up against in the beginning. If it is not acceptable, see if you can negotiate better terms with your contact. Chances are the money will be safe with a major company, but can you afford to finance their business while waiting to get paid? And on occasion, there have been major failures of large corporations—like Federated Department Stores (Macy's), TWA, Continental Airlines, and a number of major steel firms.

Invoice Accurately and Promptly

Once the sale has been made or the work completed, you need to make sure an invoice is issued. You can't get paid until you bill, so taking extra time before you do that makes no sense at all. Customers often cycle payments on invoice dates rather than transaction dates, so your slowness gives them extra time. That is the opposite of what you want.

If you are working on a large job that will be completed over a period of time, you will not want to wait before seeing any payments. Perhaps you can negotiate for a deposit. Or your deal may call for progress payments; that is, you will bill on the basis of the percentage of the work completed, not all at once at the end.

Double-check your invoices. Description of items or work performed should be complete so there is no misunderstanding. With computerized billing you should not have any math errors, but take care to be sure that your pricing is billed as agreed and that any freight that is charged has also been agreed to. Allow as little room for questions and disputes as possible; each question will delay payments and leave you with a cash flow problem. Care up front can minimize this problem.

Track Your Receivables

At least once a month, more often if you have many transactions, you should have a report called receivables aging. This lists each customer and all outstanding invoices by how old they are. It looks like this:

Customer	Amount Due			
	1–30 days	31–60 days	61–90 days	more than 90 days
ABC Corp.	$1,000		$3,000	
XYZ Company		$1,500		$500
Total	**$6,000**			

This shows two companies owing a total of $6,000, with $3,500 more than 60 days old from date of invoice. This will alert you that your invoices are not being paid as quickly as you need them to be and that something must be done.

You should start by sending monthly statements to every customer detailing what invoices they have open and for how long. If an invoice is getting old, circle it and write a short reminder. Let your customer know that you are paying attention and plan to follow up. Some companies actually wait to get asked before they will pay. You may want to call shortly after shipment to make sure goods were received and were acceptable. This is a service as well as a credit call.

Additional follow-up may be necessary. The next step is a past due notice. Send a direct and personal request asking to get paid. Follow that with a phone call. Stay on the line until you can talk to someone who can authorize payment or give you accurate information about what is holding up your check. Be polite, but be persistent. If you can't get through to the payment person or your contact, you may very well have reason for concern. Now may be the time for a certified letter. Document the demand for payment.

Always express your willingness to cooperate and make a deal. If full payment can't be made, partial payment is a step in the right direction. You don't want to lose a customer over the issue of payment but you don't need customers who are unwilling or unable to meet their financial obligations. A few of these and you will be in serious trouble yourself.

Do *not* negotiate reduced payment unless absolutely necessary. Not only is it bad for your bottom line, but as financial people move from company to company, they can spread your reputation as someone who will accept reduced payment.

What about Collections?

Once you realize that your customer, whatever the reason, simply is not willingly going to pay you, then you must go to the next step—collection activity. As of this moment, the business relationship is over and your interest must turn to getting the money owed you.

The first step in most instances is to turn the account over to a professional collection agency that will charge you a fee based only on recovery. The fee runs from 25 to 35 percent, depending on the value of the account. The higher the dollar amount, the lower the fee. If there is an industry-specific group credit association, that may be the best place for you to start, or you can contact a national agency that is well established and usually efficient. Or you may want to use your own attorney.

The only way to really enforce a collection demand is through the courts. If the amount is small, you may be able to take it to small claims court yourself. Once the debt is over the court's limit, which varies state by state, you will have to seek out a lawyer to do the required legal work of filing a lawsuit. You will probably be charged a percentage in addition to the filing fees, which are out of pocket. (Check your costs of suing—it may be worthwhile to lower your claim to stay in small claims court.) If you have all of the necessary documentation, you should have little problem getting a judgment.

Collecting, even with a legal judgment, is not a certainty. You must locate assets and then take action to have them confiscated to satisfy your claim. The easiest place to go is directly to the debtor's bank and present your legal right to take funds directly from your debtor's account. All of this is time consuming and requires legal assistance. Keep copies of customers' checks so you will know their banking information.

Bottom line is not to find yourself in this situation in the first place. Be careful at the beginning and diligent about avoiding these types of collection situations.

Take Your Banker to Lunch

Now is the time in your business when outside financing becomes a major component to reaching the next level, which is the growth phase. Once you have become established in the marketplace and have a customer base as a source of regular business, you want to turn your time and attention to growth and expansion. You may want to extend your product or service to a wider geographic area, achieve greater market penetration in your existing area, or expand your products or services to increase sales to your existing clientele. Any way you decide to pursue this next phase, it will take additional capital. And you are now far more bankable because you have a track record, and hopefully you have acquired some assets as well.

This is the moment when you will begin to find out whether you have made the right choice in banks and in bankers. Before the recent rush of mergers in the banking industry, the largest banks in your community were likely structured as decentralized operating units. That is, each branch maintained its own set of customers and the branch manager made a number of autonomous decisions. They developed new business and had some autonomous loan authority. However, the consolidation of banks means that in order to achieve the required financial economies, most functions are centralized, particularly loans. Often your branch manager can do little more than accept an application and then ship it to a central office, perhaps even to a different city or state for processing. The manager who used to make many of the decisions now isn't even in the decision-making loop.

In some banks, you won't even deal on a branch level with regard to loans. There are "relationship managers" who work entire territories developing new business. If you have chosen a larger institution, now you must learn as much as you can about how it operates. It is time to take your banker to lunch. You want to teach them more about you as well.

Find the "Right" Person

If you are still dealing with a smaller community-based bank, it will be easy to find out where the decisions are made. A larger bank may take a bit more research. Start at the branch level first. You may automatically be referred to the regional representative already described, who may take you to lunch! If you can, schedule some time "off campus"—out of the bank and out of your office to lessen distractions.

Good bankers are often active participants in the local business community—often belonging to the Rotary, Kiwanis, or Lion's clubs as well as local chambers of commerce and other business organizations. It is a part of their job. They will have a wealth of information about the rest of the businesses in your community, some of which might be potential new customers. Networking and personal contacts are the very best way to develop new business opportunities. Don't neglect your banker as a source of that information and perhaps as someone to get you involved so you can make your own contacts.

Good bankers should be a valuable source of business advice as well as a source of loan funds. Their skills are in all areas of financial management, and it is to your benefit to learn how to best manage your cash and invest it over the short term, mid term, and long term of your company's life *and* your own life. Your personal concerns would include 401(k)s and other retirement strategies, plus estate and trust planning.

What you are really looking for is more insight into the loan decision-making procedures at your bank. How long is the turnaround? Timing may be critical to your planning. And does the lender use credit scoring?

Credit Scoring—Meet R2D2, Your Banker

With the need to make loan processing less labor intensive and faster, many banks have gone to a credit scoring model to make loan decisions up to $250,000 and sometimes higher. Items such as your own personal credit history, the age of your company, and its current volume and profits are measured against predetermined standards; you either pass or you don't. Little human decision making here.

If that is what your bank does and you know there are problems in your own or your company's credit history, now is the time to face them and find out what alternatives you have for securing the financing you need. If you wait until the capital is needed and then apply, only to be turned down, you may miss any opportunity you have to take your business to the next level. Ask questions, know what you are up against, and deal with it in the best way possible.

Smaller banks may be able to deal with you on a more personal level. If you can meet with a manager who is also a decision maker and who either sits on the loan committee or makes direct presentations to it, you can present your story—the good and the bad—and hopefully be judged on an individual basis. In the next chapter, we will talk about that presentation. If you have had difficulties and have overcome them, there are ways to frame them so that you will be looked upon more positively. But to ignore any problems or negative reports and have them surface on their own is bound to damage your chances. This is the benefit of a preliminary meeting; you can discuss your situation candidly.

If your banking choice is a larger institution and you cannot make a personal pitch about your current circumstances and future needs, you can use the lunch as an information-gathering event. Find out if your bank has special programs such as loan funds or co-op programs with development organizations that you can use if you are less qualified as a borrower. Perhaps they would be more likely to approve a loan with an SBA guarantee. There are many ways to approach the need for borrowed capital, but you won't know unless you ask. Buying lunch for your banker is an investment worth making.

Hiring Your First Employees

You may have started out as your only "employee" or perhaps with a small core of others who were necessary to open your doors. If you were a one-person shop, it is likely that you worked very hard for long hours and without much of a break. The time comes when additional help is needed to accomplish the existing work as well as to prepare for the next level of business. Finding the right people at the right time is an extraordinarily difficult task, particularly in a full employment economy. Fewer qualified candidates are looking at a growing number of job opportunities and higher salaries are required to attract the best candidates. You see the effect all around you, "help wanted" signs in many windows and even fast food restaurants paying premium wages.

There are times when, out of mere frustration, you consider simply throwing warm bodies at the work that needs to be done, hoping that they will take some of the burden from you and perhaps your small existing staff. This is a serious mistake. Unproductive employees are a financial drain on a business and will eventually negatively impact the bottom line. Virtually all new employees are less than fully productive in their first few months of employment, so hiring someone underqualified for any job only enhances that problem. Take the time to conduct a complete search for qualified candidates and make the effort to interview as many as it takes to find the best match. Don't settle.

And, after the decision has been made, take extra care that your new employee has every opportunity available to become a successful contributor to your venture. The best way to accomplish this is to take the time to explain what is expected from them as a work outcome, what tools are available, and where and from whom help can be sought. If you are in a position to write a formal job description, that would be the best thing to do. A description should include all of the tasks, prioritizing them and establishing targeted outcomes. If a description isn't available, consider creating one together with your new employee. Make sure that all new hires understand your expectations and the company's goals. The time you take now to train employees properly will pay off later.

Learning how to choose good prospects to build your company and how to develop them into productive contributors are very key elements to your future. For many small businesses, labor is the largest single expense item, and productive labor is the critical element to success.

Take the Temperature of Your Venture

In Chapter 1, I reviewed the various ratios that are used to measure the progress of a business. These are most often used by lenders to make credit determinations but you should be using them on a regular basis to test your own progress. A quarterly review of any changes would probably be sufficient. Monthly looks could give you false readings because there are occasional variances that are not representative. Here's what you look at:

- *Current ratio.* Make sure that your current assets are sufficient to meet your current obligations. Two-to-one (assets-to-liabilities) is good, and if you have exceptionally good inventory and receivables, a lower ratio may be adequate.
- *Inventory turnover.* How many days does it take you to use or sell items in inventory? If the number of days is growing, chances are some of your inventory is not turning at all and should be sold—even at a loss—or written off. This will cause a loss on your profit and loss statement.
- *Receivable turnover ratio.* How many days does it take to collect an invoice owed to you? This is a good indication of the success of your collection policy. If the number of days is growing, you may be carrying some customers too long and some may never pay at all. This ratio represents your cash flow.
- *Accounts payable ratio.* How many days does it take you to pay a bill? If this number of days is growing, it is a sign that you are financing working capital by paying vendors late. There is a danger that vendors may begin pressuring for payments or supply lines may be interrupted.
- *Debt-to-worth ratio.* This sign of how much you are leveraged will give you an early indication if debt is growing too fast in relationship to current net worth. You want to be building equity in your business, and this ratio will measure your success at that goal.

Finances Are the Foundation—Build a Solid One

Once you have gotten to the operating phase of your business, it is easy to become sidetracked by any number of operating issues and certainly by those that drive sales. But now, as in the beginning, your financial management skills and the attention you pay to this aspect of your venture are the key elements in creating a stable platform to grow and prosper. Like the structure of a building, if left unattended and unrepaired the entire business will be far more fragile than is comfortable and than it has to be. Spend some of your time watching the numbers and acting on the clues they give you.

CASE STUDY

J.E. Industrial Distributing had a first year experience that was far different from the one Jack had originally projected. He made two major miscalculations.

1. Volume was only 60 percent of what was anticipated. A number of factors contributed to this outcome. First, several of his previous customers still had contractual agreements with his previous employer. The other problem he encountered was that as a new company, he had no proven track record. Several purchasing agents were reluctant to take the risk of changing suppliers.
2. Gross profit margins fell well under projections—coming in at 19 percent instead of 23 percent. J.E.'s purchases were not always at the most competitive price and discounts were not always maximized. In addition, J.E. often paid freight charges, which added to direct costs.

   The results from the first year looked like what follows:

Quarter	1	2	3	4	
Sales income	$600,000	$600,000	$750,000	$750,000	
Cost of sales	486,000	486,000	607,500	607,500	81%
Gross profit	114,000	114,000	142,500	142,500	19%
General and administrative expense:					
Rent	12,000	12,000	12,000	12,000	
Salaries	26,700	26,700	26,700	26,700	
Office expense	15,000	15,000	15,000	15,000	
Telephone	10,500	10,500	10,500	10,500	
Utilities	1,500	1,500	1,500	1,500	
Travel/entertainment	15,000	15,000	15,000	15,000	
Marketing	14,500	14,500	7,500	7,500	
Interest	18,000	18,000	18,000	18,000	
Owner's draw	21,000	21,000	21,000	21,000	
Total cost	134,200	134,200	127,200	127,200	
	20%	20%	18%	18%	
Profit (loss)	$(19,800)	$(19,800)	$ 15,300	$ 15,300	

Total loss for the year was 9,000

At the end of one year in business, the company was experiencing tight cash flow for a number of reasons. The primary cause was that it overpurchased new inventory, expecting a higher volume of sales and some contracts that did not materialize. Sales of $300,000 to $400,000 per month would have required inventory approximately double the amount sold. With sales of $200,000 per month, the starting inventory was excessive and strangled cash flow. In addition, customer payments were slower than anticipated, so cash was often short and vendor bills were often extended past 60 days. Suppliers had been very patient. While owner's compensation was deferred when necessary, it was expensed to account for the full cost of Jack's wages. His draw from his previous employer had been 30 percent higher; the current level represented 3 percent of actual sales, which had been his commission rate as a salesperson.

The balance sheet at the end of year one looked like this:

Assets—current	
Cash in banks	$ 21,400
Accounts receivable	365,000
Inventory	571,000
Prepaid insurance	19,000
Utility deposits	2,500
Total current assets	978,900
Vehicles	25,000
Leaseholds	35,000
	60,000
Less depreciation	9,000
	51,000
Total assets	1,029,900
Liabilities—current	
Accounts payable	566,700
Deferred wages	37,000
Notes payable—current portion	110,000
Total current liabilities	713,700
Long-term portion of loan	300,000
Total liabilities	1,013,700
Common stock	25,000
Retained earnings	(9,000)
Net equity	16,000
Total liabilities and capital	$1,029,600

For a start-up venture, this balance sheet is not bad, particularly because the current ratios show solvency—yet they do reflect the tight cash situation. Current assets had a ratio of 1.3-to-1, which is a bit low but not unreasonable for a start-up. Aggressive collection of receivables and higher turnover of inventory kept the operation moving, and most vendors were cooperative because they had great optimism for the venture. Higher volume also would lead to higher purchasing levels and lower net costs with volume discounts and prepaid freight.

Sales were the key issue so resources were committed to growth. Additional money was allocated to marketing. The first breakthrough came at the end of year two when sales grew to $3 million and operations were comfortably profitable. J.E. Industrial Distributing was about to be awarded a 1.5 million dollar contract that would put it at its goal in profitability. The only problem was how to finance the additional business.

Discussion Questions

1. Where does the budgeting factor in during the start-up phase of a business?

2. How would inventing control systems help to alleviate cash flow problems?

3. How committed should a new business be to maintaining the integrity of its pricing structure?

4. What are the elements of an effective collections policy?

How Big Can You Grow?

A billion here, a billion there—sooner or later it adds up to real money.

    —Senator Everett Dirksen

Learning Objectives

Once you have completed this chapter, you will be able to:

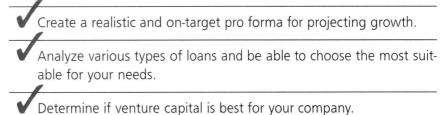

✔ Create a realistic and on-target pro forma for projecting growth.

✔ Analyze various types of loans and be able to choose the most suitable for your needs.

✔ Determine if venture capital is best for your company.

✔ Understand the advantages of strategic alliances.

✔ Explain the basics of going public to raise large sums of money.

First you preplan your business, next you open its doors, and then you learn from trial and error how to best operate it. Once you feel that you have come up to speed, you can begin to look around and determine how many opportunities there are to grow the company into a strong and successful venture. It is best to take this process step by step, because if you increase volume before you have stabilized your pricing and set up proper controls on your costs, you may find yourself with increased cash outflow, greater pressures, and little on the bottom line to show for your new volume. Growth for growth's sake isn't a desirable goal. Profitable growth is the only way to build your business. And as always, knowledgeable financial management is the primary desirable skill.

How to Finance Growth

As we have seen from the pro formas shown earlier in this book, each growth phase causes cash flow shortages. And the more rapid the growth, the more serious the potential money problems. A company growing by 50 percent annually can literally run out of capital and not be able to meet payroll and other necessary obligations. The increased costs range from the purchase of equipment and additional inventory to the operating increases in payroll, utilities, taxes, and all types of administrative costs. Controls are still important at times like these, but controls alone are insufficient to cover the capital needs. For example, a manufacturing company assuming a new contract that will expand its operation by 50 percent may be facing the following:

- Preparation of additional space
- 25 percent increase in inventory levels to maximize turnover efficiency
- Increased travel and sales expense to service the new account(s)
- Cash flow needs as follows: Assuming sales growth from $700,000 to $1,200,000, gross margins of 40 percent. Overhead costs grow from 30 percent to 33 percent. Net profit (before tax) of 7 percent. Sales on credit with a 32-day cash turnaround.

Year one looks like this:

Quarter	1	2	3	4
Sales income	175,000	250,000	350,000	425,000
Direct expense	105,000	150,000	210,000	255,000
Gross Profit	70,000	100,000	140,000	170,000
Less general and administrative expense	65,100	93,000	131,600	158,100
Net (before tax)	4,900	7,000	8,400	11,900
Beginning cash		(20,100)	(88,100)	(169,700)
Plus collections	150,000	175,000	250,000	350,000
Total available	150,000	154,900	161,900	190,300
Less direct costs	105,000	150,000	210,000	255,000
Less general and administrative expense	65,100	93,000	131,600	158,100
Total expense	170,100	243,000	341,600	413,100
Ending cash	(20,100)	(88,100)	(169,700)	(222,700)

As you can see, the cash shortage problem started to escalate during the second quarter and became critical by the end of the year. This is without even accounting for the extra expense of site preparation, inventory level increases, and overhead expenses. Without an outside source of additional capital, growth could actually destroy this company.

It is possible to make up some of the shortfall through vendor credit and possible long-term dating on invoices but certainly not the entire amount, which might well exceed $300,000 before this phase draws to a close. The time has come to approach some source of outside financing to seek the funds required to proceed. Step one of this process is determining exactly how much you will require. You are likely to tie up all of your collateral on this new financing so going back to get more money later will be virtually impossible.

On-Target Pro Formas

There are a large number of software programs that will help you do an easy pro forma. Plug in a few numbers, and in mere seconds a document appears that *looks* professional and creditable, but *is* it? In general terms, this pro forma will be a good guideline, but in a situation like a one-shot chance at financing, it is unlikely to be accurate enough.

The question is how to improve your projections and make sure you have determined exactly how much money you will need. The answer is to construct a customized hybrid format. That is, you may use one of the common software programs as a platform—an Excel spreadsheet will do just fine—then research and review each number as you put it in. Do not just plug in some assumptions and then run a statement based on loosely structured percentages.

For example, the wrong way is to

- use your current sales figure and plug in your goal as percentage growth.
- assume that direct costs will stay the same.
- use fixed numbers as overhead expense and come up with a healthy net profit based solely on untested theories of the effect of higher volume.

However, the right way to look at these issues is to

- construct a sales analysis based on current numbers less any assumed and natural loss of business.
- add the value of new customers or contracts that have been developed.
- add a conservative projection of new business you will win.
- give every category a dollar value and be specific.
- account for seasonal variations. In short, use real numbers.

Direct Expense

- Will you have to increase your inventory of raw material or finished goods to serve your new customers? Will the expense of inventory go up as a percentage?
- Do you need new equipment to produce more goods? Can you find good used equipment at a good price? Can you find labor saving devices and actually lower the cost of direct labor?

  A restaurant I worked with several years ago grew enough to be able to purchase an automatic pasta machine and ultimately cut 30 hours of labor per week.

Fixed Costs

- Will the rent stay the same or is greater space needed for expansion or storage?
- Will the cost of utilities go up by the same percentage as the growth?
- Do you expect that you will need to increase administrative staff?
- Will benefits have to be raised to attract and retain the caliber of employees that are required by a growing concern?
- What sales staff is required to maintain new accounts?
- Will you increase your marketing expense to continue to build new volume to enhance this period of growth?

You should ask these and any other individual questions you can think of. If the answers involve getting quotes or estimates from outside sources such as insurance companies, do so. Create a document that reflects the most accurate representation of your future business situation. After all, you need to know precisely how much money you will require—and you don't want to underestimate the number. Armed with this data, you are ready to begin looking for your financing.

Structuring the Right Loan

You are already ahead of the game of borrowing when you know the exact amount you need. The next phase is to match the type and the term of the loan with the cash flow needs of the business. These depend on the use of the money and the expected payback, that is, how long it will take for you to realize the benefit of the financing. You may choose to borrow money in one of the following ways:

- Short term—less than one year
- Intermediate term—as long as three to five years
- Long term—in excess of five years

Short-Term Loans

Generally, this will be a line of credit that you may draw on as needed. It may be used as working capital to smooth out short-term cash needs, such as financing a large contract that pays when it is complete, or for a seasonal increase in volume. If the growth is continual, one year is not likely to be sufficient for the use of outside capital.

A revolving line of credit allows you to draw down a portion or all of the line when you require it and pay down any amount when the funds are available. If you have a $100,000 line and need $25,000 to fund payroll and $30,000 to pay vendors, you simply make a draw. When your receivables are paid, then you pay off the line. Most of these loans have language that requires you to pay down the loan to zero for up to 30 days each year. In our high growth scenario, this would be impossible. However, in many instances, these lines are renewed without the pay down for several years, each time on a one-year basis.

A line of credit is not the way to go to purchase equipment that will create future profits. If the payback is not short term, the loan cannot be either.

Intermediate-Term Loans

A three-year to five-year debt is normally written as an installment loan rather than a line of credit. You may be purchasing a new piece of equipment or updating an entire department and will need the full amount of the loan at one time. Once the improvement or equipment is in place, increased revenue and increased profits are expected, and those proceeds will be utilized for debt service. Your loan will carry a regular monthly payment and the term should be set to coincide with the payback on the improvements purchased.

There is also a hybrid revolving loan that is normally intermediate in term and is called a nonrevolving line of credit. When you will use the money over a period of time—to fund a serious capital expansion or perhaps some long-term contract growth, the money is not needed all at once. As the money is being drawn over a period of up to a year, interest payments are made only on the portion that has been drawn. Once the draw is complete, the loan terms for the balance of the time and regular installment payments begin.

Long-Term Loans

The primary reason for acquiring a loan of more than five years is to undertake a very substantial business expansion or acquisition. This often includes property and improvements and the purchase of major equipment. This type of investment will take some time to return any payback, so up to ten or more years are often required. Mortgages can be written for up to 20 years.

This type of lending is at least partially speculative because the long-term projections of any business are based on assumptions that could change over the years. The business cycles have shortened substantially in recent years due to major changes in technology and markets. Many banks are more reluctant to loan beyond five to seven years, and few will go beyond five years for working-capital loans. The SBA, however, may guarantee a seven-year working-capital loan; having that guarantee will ease the exposure of the bank.

When deciding what type and term loan meets the financing need for your business, look at a mixed loan package as well. Consider a mid-term installment loan to purchase or upgrade equipment and beef up inventory, and a one-year line of credit to smooth out cash flow for other expenses. Our 50 percent growth company shown earlier in this chapter could use a $200,000 term loan and a $100,000 credit line to fund the year of rapid growth.

Special Loans

Accounts receivable financing. There are two distinct types of loans that are used to finance growing accounts receivable. One is a line of credit based on the amount of your receivables and collateralized by them. As your receivables grow so does the loan, and as they are paid off the loan amount is reduced.

You will not be able to borrow on 100 percent of the value of your accounts. The average is about 80 percent due to various conditions the bank may put on eligible accounts. You will have to turn in an aging report of your receivables on a regular basis, and it is likely that any account older than 60 days will go into the ineligible category and reduce the amount of money you can borrow. You can see why you must be diligent about collecting the money owed to you.

This type of loan can go on for a long time and never be paid back to zero. It will generally cost you more than an "off the shelf" loan by 2–6 percent, due to the higher cost of the monitoring that is required.

The other way to raise money from the value of your receivables is to sell them to a factor. A factor is a person or a company that will advance cash to you when the sale is made, and the monies will be paid back directly to the factor. The factor will be responsible for collecting the accounts rather than you. The credit decisions on this type of financing will be based on the creditworthiness of your customers, not of your business. The cost of this type of financing can be very high, and you have little control over how your customers are handled. Keep in mind that some factors are very forceful about collections, which may offend your customers.

Inventory Financing. Large-ticket items such as furniture, appliances, and automobiles are sometimes directly financed by the lending institution. When the item is sold, the loan is paid down.

The cost of this type of loan is also a bit high, due to the cost of the monitoring. However, this may be offset by discounts offered by suppliers for fast payment.

There are other unique loan products and some combinations that you can coordinate with your banker. Make sure you line up sufficient capital to fund what you need and leave enough time to pay it back without a struggle.

Getting Your Banker to Say Yes

First, remember that your banker really wants to say yes. Her business is making loans, and if she turns down all potential customers, there will be precious little in the way of profit for the bank. But your banker also wants to make a fairly secure loan and to feel confident that it will be paid back in a timely fashion. Your job is to convince her that you are a good candidate.

Part of what you need to accomplish this is sufficient knowledge and confidence to demonstrate that you know how to run a profitable business. Your previous track record will speak in part to that question. Your reason for requesting the loan will also tell your banker about the management of your company. Make sure you are asking for a feasible loan. The issues to consider are:

- Is the company making a profit sufficient to meet debt service?
- Does the loan amount seem adequate to meet the stated business goals?
- Does the loan term make sense in relation to the cash flow projections? That is, will the increased cash flow be available in the same time frame?
- Is there currently sufficient collateral to back the loan, or can it be secured by the increase in receivables and assets, such as inventory, that will result from the loan?

If you have done your homework, you will know how your bank makes loan decisions. If you are borderline, securing an SBA guarantee may be enough to make the deal work.

If you are dealing with one of the larger banking institutions, it is almost assured that it is an SBA Preferred Lender, which means that it can designate your loan as an SBA loan, and it doesn't need the approval of that agency. If you are told that it does not handle SBA loans or that the SBA has turned you down, you are not getting the whole story. Don't be afraid to ask for details; you have a right to them.

The circumstances will change at a small community bank. Loans will be approved by the loan committee and you will need to supply your own paperwork in addition to filling out the bank's application. Loans are based on the following four criteria:

1. *Purpose.* Is the purpose of the loan to make an investment in something that will cause future revenue and profit growth for the company? Few if any banks will lend money to pay back old debt because there will be no ongoing stream of profits to meet debt service. The lender looks to

the future of your business because that's where its payback will come from.

2. *Payment.* Here is where your pro formas become very important. Can you show that after the money has been received and utilized that the company has expectations of positive cash flow to meet future obligations? It may not be there immediately, but once you have completed the projected growth, cash flow should be catching up.

3. *Protection.* Do you now have or will you be acquiring the assets to secure the loan? If the company is undersecured, can you, as the principal, provide additional private security (such as a second mortgage on property) that will collateralize the loan? Your personal guarantee will likely be needed as well.

4. *People.* Your level of expertise as well as that of those around you will be called into play. Your personal credit history may also come into play here, but your business experience is a critical factor in the deal. If your banker isn't aware of your accomplishments, don't be shy. Make sure you have included data about yourself in your documentation. You want to increase the banker's level of confidence in you.

The answer to getting your banker to say yes is a fairly simple one: find out exactly what makes your banker do so. What is she looking for in a good loan? Remember that your bank wants to accept your proposal, so put together your plan and documentation meeting its criteria. Unless you have some major problem in your history, you can make yourself bankable. And if you are candid about past problems, you may be able to overcome them as well. Explain any situation you faced, why it happened, and how it has been corrected. You never want your bank to find out bad news on its own.

Private Investors

Most financially astute business owners will finance their companies using more than one source of capital. Seldom is all of the money you require available from a single source, so being creative is more likely to get you all of the capital you need to take your business to the next level. Let's assume that you have been in business for a while and are beginning to see some real growth at a reasonable profit, and you have borrowed some money from the bank. But you need more and you know you can't go back to negotiate a larger loan. Next step? How about a new equity partner?

Assuming that your legal structure will permit it (normally a Sub S Corporation will), you can approach individuals and offer them a piece of the company for an investment. You are selling off shares that currently belong to you, but in the end, the increased capital will make the company and your remaining shares that much more valuable, particularly if you can now achieve the growth potential you project.

There are some limitations for an existing company that has bank loans in place. If you sell an interest in excess of 20 percent of the company, you will have to disclose that fact to the bank and there is a good chance that the minority shareholder would have to become a coguarantor on your loans. A potential investor may not want that additional liability.

Having minority shareholders is really not much of a problem to a small, closely held company. The business is still controlled and operated by the majority partner, and the primary benefit to the minority shareholders is financial. They can share in profits to the degree that a dividend is declared, and their shares will increase in value to the degree that the company increases in value. When and if the company is sold, they will realize this appreciation in value. Frankly, the benefits are primarily on the side of the majority holder.

So why would anyone invest in a closely held company? The answer is that sophisticated investors will only do so under very controlled circumstances that give them some assurance of a return. Less experienced investors may think that they are buying more than is really there, or they may just be in it for the prestige of ownership. This is often true of restaurant investors; people seem to want to own a piece of a popular restaurant.

You must make the determination of what type of investor you are looking for. The best is someone who understands the risk and can afford to lose the money they are investing. A professional in another field may be the perfect candidate. Accepting a first-time investor in a small company may be a serious mistake because his expectations may be unrealistic and could cause serious problems for both of you down the line. If the expected results don't occur, your new "partner" might become overly troublesome, even to the degree of taking legal action. His rights are limited, but that won't stop the distraction.

The best way to attract and satisfy an outside investor is to be open and straightforward about what you need in terms of dollars; what sort of return the investment will bring and when; in what way, if any, the investment can be bought out; and on what basis it will be valued. The advantage to you is that you are paying a return based on the results of the business so that during difficult times, there will not be a cash burden as there is with a bank loan, which is due no matter how tight money gets. Plus, you don't have to return the principal investment until the company is financially strong. In fact, your bank may control what you pay out as long as you have outstanding loans, so check out your loan agreement terms.

Using Venture (or Vulture) Capital

If your capital needs exceed $250,000, and if the return on the investment of that money is expected to be fairly high, you may be a candidate for venture capital. The businesses that are most interesting to venture firms are those in high-tech areas where there are patents or software copyrights that may become quite valuable. Companies that hold a trademark with market awareness or intellectual property that gives them a proprietary edge also are good candidates.

You may be eligible even if your collateral is insufficient for lenders, or if you operated at a loss during the early stages and the company's future, while interesting to a savvy businessperson, is still too risky for a traditional lender. Many of the very successful high-tech companies have been started or maintained through the growth stage with the help of venture capital.

However, venture capital is an investment, not a loan. The money is at risk on the success of your venture just like the money you personally have put in along the way. If your company succeeds at what it is currently doing, the venture capitalist will own a good portion of that success. The capitalist will be your partner in many ways so be careful when choosing one.

The good news here is that most of the individuals or groups that have started venture capital companies have been in business long enough to evaluate whether your concept and its proposed market have the potential you believe they do and whether you are headed toward realizing some of that potential. They can share your vision, which will get you attention and perhaps real tangible offers. You will have to create a far more complete financial package than you would have to for your bank because you must now describe and document your assumptions about where you are headed. This business plan will be read and understood.

How to Find a Venture Capital Firm

Whereas banks advertise and have branches all around, you will have to do research to find a venture capital firm. Here are some ways to find candidates:

- *Look at your industry.* Finding a firm that is already active in your industry may give you some advantage because it will be up to speed about your potential, as well as about the problems you face. Ask other early stage companies or inquire through your trade association.

- *Talk to your banker.* Venture capital firms have banking relationships for their own activities, so your local banker may have recommendations of firms she has worked with.
- *Check universities.* Through graduate schools of business or Small Business Development Centers you may find a list of active firms.
- *Search the Internet.* A simple search for "venture capital" with virtually any search engine will provide a substantial number of sites for you to review, many of them geographically specific. You don't need to approach only local firms, however.
- *Ask for a referral.* If you still don't know where to start, find just a single firm to start with and ask them about others in your area or in the industry. You will likely get quite a few names. Currently there is almost $30 billion in investment capital in play, and that is a large field to mine. You can find several competent players if you look.

Understand that This Will Take Time

If you need money to meet day-to-day operations now, you probably don't have the luxury of time to find and work with a venture capital firm. After you have found a few likely candidates (and you should seek out more than one), you must make a full presentation to them explaining your entire operation. Then there will be time in negotiating the deal (remember—this is an investment), and creating and signing the documents. The whole process could take months. So if you know that you are not likely to be bankable and you still will need a substantial amount of capital, the time to seek and prepare to approach a venture capital firm is far in advance of the time the funds will be needed.

Approaching the Venture Capital Firm

Early in the process, asking to partner with a venture capital firm is a pure numbers game. You create a short background piece about your business, its history, and its goals and submit it for preliminary consideration. A two or three page executive summary should suffice. Include information about your product or service and the market you are seeking to reach. Describe how you started and how far you have gotten in your business plan to this point. Be as specific as you can about what amount of capital you are looking for and what type of return you think it will bring. You should know that most venture firms expect to triple their money over a period of around five years, counting both profit payouts and equity growth. They are taking a risk. Because they will lose on some ventures, they need a high return on successful investments to offset their losses.

The better firms will receive hundreds of requests, most of which are inappropriate. Firms usually are very specific in their criteria, so you will know soon if they are interested in further information to evaluate. Rejection at this round occurs at a high rate and is normally swift.

On to the Dog-and-Pony Show

If the firm you query has further interest, you will be asked to submit a complete proposal. Your end will take a good bit of work and it will be scrutinized thoroughly on the other end. Some of the elements you will need to include are:

- a complete company history from day one—how your business began and how it has progressed.
- a description of the concept of your product or service, how much it has been developed to date, and what opportunities exist for this and other products or services that might spring from your work.

- an in-depth analysis of the potential market and what competing products, if any, already exist.
- your sales and marketing strategy showing that you know how to bring your goods to a competitive market and capitalize on opportunities.
- a complete list of all involved executives and innovators including yourself, with your business histories, areas of expertise, and special skills.
- your financials to date, including your most recent tax returns. Development losses won't scare venture capitalists; they are expected in new businesses. Many of the largest Internet companies have yet to make a profit, yet they are highly capitalized on future potential. But poor financial structure and unfunded debt to vendors or taxing bodies will concern the firm. If you have these problems, you may want to resolve them before submitting a full proposal. If you had problems in the past, be sure you explain how you resolved them and how you intend to prevent a recurrence.
- financial projections—as well documented as you can make them—with demographic information and competitor data.
- your proposal for how much money you need and how it will be returned. Will you pay a percentage return each year and then return the initial investment with a premium over a set period? What is the total return you are offering and how soon do you expect to return the principal? Many firms have limits as to how long they wish to be invested in a company. If your plans match theirs, you could benefit. Make sure your pro formas account for your payout to investors—you can't just promise it, you must prove it.

You Must Make a Presentation

Venture capitalists, perhaps even more than most bankers, know that they are backing the entrepreneur as well as the venture. You will have to meet with them in person for a complete presentation of what you have included in your business proposal. Make sure that you are knowledgeable about all aspects of your business and proposal, even if you didn't personally write some of the sections. Bring along the whole team that is responsible for the company: show off your talent.

You are trying to sell this investor on something that you clearly believe in yourself, so it is great to show your own enthusiasm, but don't try to oversell. Your audience is very sophisticated and has heard great promises before. You will win them with sincerity and facts. Bring along as much documentation as you can put together. Make it a convincing presentation. Prepare yourself to answer any and all questions as honestly as you can, deferring to others from your organization when the questions are in their area of expertise. Practice and polish your presentation; the stakes are high and success is worth it.

Make the Right Deal with the Right Firm

In addition to capital, many of these firms offer management expertise. With some firms that is a very important element, but with others the intrusion will cause more problems than you need. These are people you are going to be involved with for a number of years and with whom you will work closely at times. Choose them as you would choose any new partner—very carefully. You have the right (and the responsibility) to scrutinize them as thoroughly as they are scrutinizing you.

- Are they bringing special expertise to the deal that enhances it?
- Is their financial track record good? For example, have they been involved with too many failures or struggles for control?
- Where is their capital coming from, and will your project be fully funded?
- Do you know all the players on their team? Who will be your primary contact?

The relationship between a venture capital firm and your company is a lot closer and more personal than that between you and your bank. It has an investment, a stake, and often a personal interest. The effect of all of that can be very positive, and usually is, but there are times when you become at odds and the company suffers. The firm will exercise their due diligence on your business; you should not get so caught up in the money side that you don't look clearly at them as well.

Other Strategic Alliances

Forming partnerships with individuals and other companies for specific purposes is another way to grow your existing company without shouldering the full capital burden. If you can develop a new product with the financial assistance of the material supplier, won't that be a good idea?

Perhaps you need more space but you can't finance an entire building, and that's more than you need now anyway. Join forces with someone who is in the same situation and jointly develop property you can both use.

You can partner with your customers to be their sole supplier for certain products in return for maintaining a higher level of inventory, faster delivery, and better service on your part. You then take that contract to the source supplier (the primary manufacturer) and ask them to partner with you on your inventory needs, perhaps on consignment or on invoice dating. Everyone benefits in a situation like this. Your customers get what they need and you and your supplier get additional or steadier business.

For example, a graphic designer moved her office into a mid size printing company. It utilized her as its inside design department and she utilized it as her primary printer. She had use of cheap space (it was readily available), the use of the printer's better equipment, and good referrals. In return, the printer gained a department that it didn't have to pay when work wasn't needed, but she was on site when her expertise was required.

For another example, a large construction job was being bid, and one contractor who had the inside track was concerned that the size of the job represented too big a risk. He joined forces with another company about the same size, and they formed a joint venture for the purpose of completing the job. They shared the work, the financing, and the profits. It worked so well that they formed alliances for other projects later.

Not all outcomes are so wonderful, but a well thought out alliance or partnership can really work in the building years of a company. You must have a full discussion of all of the obligations and expectations of your arrangement. Construct performance agreements and state how you'll share financing requirements and profits. Create a written contract. Each partner should use its own lawyer to protect all concerned. Some alliance issues are:

- *Term of agreement.* Is it for one project or a set period?
- *Price or cost limits.* Where there is a joint agreement to supply, there should be a pricing stipulation that protects both parties. Where there is joint development, cost limits are needed. Each side must agree not to assume obligations in the name of the partnership beyond a certain dollar limit without permission of the other(s).
- *Performance standards.* Whatever benchmarks are critical to the success of the project should be written into the agreement. Remedies for failure to perform must also be stated.
- *Causes of termination.* Indicate the circumstances under which the partnership can be dissolved and the implications on the partnership's financial and contractual obligations.

The key to a winning partnership or alliance is a shared vision. A good synergy can propel both sides to the next level. Clarify terms to prevent misunderstandings. If you anticipate ending up in a dispute, don't form the alliance. No one but the lawyers win in disputes.

Going Public

Everyone is in awe of the amount of money that Bill Gates makes from his share of Microsoft. On a bad day on the stock market, he loses more than most of us will ever see in a lifetime. His wealth is awesome and it is attractive but it is surely not for everyone. Nor is it something that many can aspire to.

It takes time, it takes money, and it takes the help of a lot of people to take a company public.

It would be impossible to cover all of the considerations of a public offering in one chapter of a book. Because this book is for entrepreneurs, I am assuming that by the time you are seriously considering going public, you will have many financial and tax advisors in place. What I will do here is give you an overview of what going public means so you can consider if you even want to attempt it.

Most small and closely-held mid-size companies find most of their capital in the debt market; that is, they use loans. This will limit the amount of capital the companies can secure to the value of their assets and their projected cash flow. Due to these limits, their growth may be limited as well. Going public allows a higher amount of capital to flow into the business from the equity, rather than debt, market. The amount of capital may be substantial, and if the company continues to grow and prosper, additional financing is far easier to obtain if it has gone public.

The Benefits to the Owner

During the initial public offering (IPO) the previous equity holders get to cash in their chips. The issue price of a new stock may be set as high as ten times its current value so the founders and anyone else holding an equity interest will see a tremendous increase in the value of that equity. For founders, it is one of the only ways to cash out of their own venture at an early stage and still be able to participate in the future of the company. And the founders will no longer be held liable for any corporate loans or debts.

Companies intending to go public at some time in their early life may also have issued stock to key employees as a way to attract and retain them. When the day comes that the stock is publicly traded, these employees can cash in as well. In addition to making Bill Gates and Paul Allen billionaires, Microsoft has helped a vast number of other company employees become millionaires, some at a very young age.

After the offering, the ability to grant stock options in a publicly-traded company is quite an incentive in attracting new talent. The company can grow large enough to have a pool of talent around instead of just the founders and perhaps a few loyal followers. When Steve Jobs built Apple Corporation, it was limited to almost a small cult of believers. The company he came back to turn around was very professional, with a cadre of talented managers.

Remember, however, that after Apple went public, Jobs was forced to leave by the new management group, which had a different vision for the company. Because he no longer had outright control, like any other CEO of a public company, he served at the will of the board. Some other founders have left under equally difficult circumstances. What does this mean to you?

Consider the Challenges and the Disadvantages of Going Public

It would be difficult to identify the greatest challenge of a public offering; there are three challenges, and they are equally tough.

1. It is time consuming.
2. It takes a great deal of work.
3. It costs a good bit of money.

And there is no guarantee you will be successful. Some companies that work very hard at going public never get there. Look at the three issues in depth:

The time. Few founders have completed the steps required to offer stock to the public in less than six months, and some have taken up to a full year. Beginning with the internal work on the business plan and records, continuing with the registration with various agencies and the SEC, and finally getting to the opening day, each task is time consuming, and the founders often do not have total control over when the other parties involved will finish their work. The wheels of government regulatory bodies often grind slowly.

There is a tremendous challenge in creating a business concept that has the staying power of one year when the funds are not there and your attention is focused elsewhere. In the interim, technology can change, markets might fluctuate, and competition may move in first.

The effort. It is almost a second full-time job to ready a company for a public filing. There are actually two businesses going on at once, the one you are financing and the one set up to get the financing in place. You begin by completing perhaps the most comprehensive business plan you have ever done. One of the hallmarks of a public offering is full disclosure, so all the documents your business produces must be complete in every respect.

Then you must put together your team of professionals, who will lead you through the maze of regulations and filings. Accountants must audit the company financial records, attorneys will complete and file paperwork, consultants and underwriters will advise and will handle the offering, and a public relations firm will make sure that your public profile is positive and that you have a high profile in the media.

And you will be in the middle of all of this, managing your "team," completing your assigned tasks, perhaps meeting with regulators from the SEC, and meeting with the media to drum up interest in your offering. Plus you may still have your principal business to run.

Everything about your company will become part of the public record, including your salary and benefits. What you may have considered proprietary information will now be in the public domain. Chances are that it won't damage your venture but you are right to have a passing concern. If there have been past internal transactions that may be questionable, clean them up before you start the process of making an offering.

Last but not the least, the cost. You are trying to raise money to fund a business venture and expand it to a higher level of success. What you should know about the public offering is that the cost can take from 25 to 35 percent of the total offering. A $10 million offering may net the company less than $7 million. There is a good bit of work to pay for.

The largest line item expense will be the commission paid to the underwriter, which will range from 8 to 10 percent. In addition, there are the additional underwriting out-of-pocket expenses that must be paid. This may total approximately $300,000 (on the same $10 million offering). One-third, or $100,000, will be paid when you sign a letter of intent, and this amount is nonrefundable even if the offering is never made.

Your professional fees will be substantial as well, with legal fees leading the way in a range of $50–200,000 needed for the review of all corporate transactions and all disclosures and to complete the filings. Accounting fees will depend on the audit history of the company and they can range from $10–100,000. Even the printing of all the documents, disclosures, and offering prospectuses can cost more than $50,000! And don't forget there are filing and registration fees to pay.

You will incur nonrefundable expenses all along the way, even if you are not successful in getting the stock offering to the market.

Before you start, consider the risk and measure it against the potential reward.

Wrap-Up

There is no doubt that growing a business is an expensive proposition. It takes a good bit of capital to keep the momentum going beyond the breakeven point and ultimately into long-term sustainable profitability. For most businesses, sourcing this funding in an adequate amount and in a timely manner is a real challenge. You would be smart to consider all the alternatives and perhaps utilize more than one. A combination of investment, loans, and joint venturing may well give you what you need with the varying terms that will make it easier to meet your obligations. You will be prepared as well for the next round of opportunities.

Make your decisions along the way with a long-term plan in mind. Don't just run from crisis to crisis with a stopgap funding plan that meets this week's payroll but leaves you with little idea of how next month's bills will be met. Learn how to do pro formas, and more importantly, learn how to use them.

In the end, you want to be successful enough to make proactive decisions instead of reacting to circumstances. And you want stability whether you decide to keep the company or go public.

CASE STUDY

Year two had been a successful one in tightening up the balance sheet, a necessity if new capital was to be secured. The company was only two years into the original loan and now the need was for a revolving line of credit to finance growth.

The year two balance sheet looked like this:

Cash in banks	$ 45,000
Accounts receivable	405,000
Inventory	400,000
Prepaid insurance	12,000
Utility deposits	1,500
Total current assets (1)	863,500
Vehicles	25,000
Leaseholds	35,000
Total	60,000
Less depreciation	18,000
	42,000
Total assets	905,500
Liabilities—current	
Accounts payable	395,000
Deferred wages	21,000
Notes payable—current portion	110,000
Total current liabilities (2)	526,000
Long-term portion of loan	202,000
Total liabilities	720,000
Common stock	25,000
Retained earnings	152,500
Net equity	177,500
Total liabilities and capital	$905,500

Note the current assets (1) at $863,500 and current liabilities (2) at $526,000. The ratio was at about 1.6-to-1 (1.6 of asset for every 1 of liability), which was a substantial improvement sure to impress any banker. This was achieved by reducing inventory levels and putting the capital directly into lowering payables. The business was running far more efficiently. Vendors were being paid more promptly and everything was in place for securing additional financing.

New sales of approximately $150,000 per month were expected, requiring at least 60 days inventory of $240,000 (based on 80 percent cost of two months sales of 300,000). These sales would become receivables and turn into cash, so a revolving line of credit for $300,000 would be more than enough to fund this growth. The increased purchasing power would also lower unit costs, and profits would meet the 23 percent original projection. The sales and gross profit volume were also likely to meet the start-up pro forma. However, by now the overhead costs were higher and the net profit lower.

The third year results looked like the following:

Sales	$4,600,000	
Cost of sales	3,522,000	77%
Gross profit	1,078,000	
General and administrative expense		
Rent	60,000	
Salaries[1]	300,000	
Office expense[2]	90,000	
Telephone	35,000	
Utilities	9,000	
Travel/entertainment[3]	72,000	
Marketing	50,000	
Interest	65,000	
Owner's draw	150,000	
Miscellaneous[4]	40,000	
Total administrative cost	871,000	
Profit (before tax)	$ 207,000	4.6%

[1] Staffing levels had increased to three administrative staff, two truck drivers, and two outside salespeople.

[2] Office expense included outside contractors including a payroll service and purchase of a computer system, which was expensed.

[3] Travel to all major conventions were now budgeted and all salespeople had entertainment budgets.

[4] This included employee benefits and truck expense.

Discussion Questions

1. Would you have employed a different strategy to tighten up the operation from year one to year two?

2. What weaknesses do you see?

3. Are the ratios where they should be?

4. Are there other strategic moves that should be implemented?

CHAPTER

Cash Cow or Dying Bovine?

The stars might lie but the numbers never do.

—Recorded by Mary Chapin Carpenter

Learning Objectives

Once you have completed this chapter, you will be able to:

✔ Identify the signs of a cash cow and understand how to milk one.

✔ Establish the best investment strategies for excess cash.

✔ Determine the signs of trouble in a mature business.

✔ Create an effective turnaround strategy.

✔ Understand the basics of Chapter 11 Reorganization.

From the days of start-up through the rest of the life of a business, conditions never remain static. They are always in a state of change. Internal operations begin in a fairly loose way until knowledge and experienced aid in tightening them up. Markets begin virtually untapped until your products or services win a level of acceptance and your company becomes recognized. And just when you think you have the situation well in hand, it is time to reinvent the business.

At one time, the business cycles that were experienced over the life of a company extended for a period of 10–15 years or longer. Currently, with the rapidly changing technology and new market delivery systems, plus the impact of global markets, the cycles are less than 6–8 years. What wasn't even imagined just a few years ago, such as selling on the Internet, is now a reality.

For some companies the changes offer new opportunities, and they take advantage of them. Others find themselves in a difficult place. Knowing where you are and what the options are is the major element to mastering your current business circumstance.

Identifying a True Cash Cow

Perhaps your established business has found itself in a very interesting position in your business cycle. The good news is that your company is stable, fairly profitable, and not difficult to maintain. The other side of the coin is that the future (farther than three to five years) looks fairly uncertain unless a major reengineering of your product or your market is undertaken. If your business meets some of the following criteria, you may be running a cash cow—a business that makes good profit but has a short life span left. Here are several of the primary indicators:

- *The industry is mature.* Your product or service is one that has been established for a long time. Most potential customers either have what you are selling or have decided that the next generation of products is of more interest. Let's take, for example, the VCR and rental movies. They are likely to be replaced soon by computer-downloaded movies. So shortly there will be few new customers for VCR or rental movies. Some products that are almost obsolete (mostly industrial products) are also in this category—products sold to the shrinking steel and auto industries, for example.

- *No appreciable new growth has taken place for the last few years.* For reasons already established above, there are few new customers and few new sales. Units and dollars have remained flat or perhaps even gone down. All revenue growth has resulted from pricing increases.
- *No new players are entering the business.* This may be because of the small and shrinking market, or more likely, because the high level of capital investment is impossible to justify to an aspiring entrepreneur in this industry. You will notice that competition is shrinking not growing. Consolidation is everywhere.
- *No capital investment is required for your current business.* Your company already has all of the tools it needs to satisfy existing market demand. The equipment may not be the most modern, but it is serviceable, and very little else is available that would improve profitability. Anyway, by any serious analysis, new equipment wouldn't be cost effective.

If this sounds something like the current situation in your company, you may be leading what is sometimes referred to as a cash cow. It is also assumed that you are profitable and have been for some time (the past 2-4 years). And every indication you can read is that you will continue to be profitable in the near-term future. Perhaps your best business strategy is to milk your current position for all it is worth because the life of this venture is limited. If demand is flat or even diminishing, the time will come when there isn't sufficient volume to make a profit. Until that time, you can do fairly well and make other plans for your next venture. Some things to consider:

- A market without much competition is *not* a price sensitive market. Do some experimentation with price increases until you determine if there is any resistance. You may be able to expand your operating margins even farther with pricing adjustments and drop more dollars to the bottom line.

- You must watch your overhead costs closely because you will not see the percentage costs of your fixed expenses go down as the result of volume growth as you would expect from a growing business. Any cost increases you allow at this point will simply shrink your profit.

- You can't improve the long-term prospects of businesses like this by making changes around the margins. If you choose to commit to a different product or service in order to move to a more vibrant sector of the economy, you will have to revamp the company completely. It may be more cost effective to build a new business from the ground up than try to alter an operating company with existing debt and excess baggage in terms of equipment and maybe personnel expertise.

Perhaps the most astute way to milk a cash cow is to run it hard and efficiently for as long as you can and use the excess profits you can make from this type of situation to invest in other opportunities.

The way not to do it is to become complacent (because running a cash cow seems easy) and spend all the profits frivolously as if they will come in forever; they won't.

Investing Excess Cash

Whether you are operating a cash cow or a business that occasionally has times when earnings are in excess of need, you want to put your money to work for you. There are a number of options and a number of ways to increase the financial efficiency of your company. Here are some ideas:

Reinvest the Cash

Reinvest the cash in creating better buying opportunities for your company. There are a number of ways to increase your bottom line with your excess cash. One is to take advantage of any "prompt pay" discounts that may be offered by your vendors. You may be able to get a reduction of 2–3 percent off your invoices by paying in ten days. Depending on the cash flow needs of your supplier, they may be willing to deal. Ask.

Buy product and material in larger quantities and ask for an additional discount as well as prepaid freight. Large orders require less handling and so they are of greater value to your vendors. You should make sure that your vendors pass at least a part of that value to you.

Look for special overstock offers that come up from time to time. These are more often seen at the end of seasons or the end of the year. Some states have a floor tax on inventory that they assess at the end of the year. This is a serious incentive to move goods. Why not be there to make a deal?

Make inquiries within your industry, including among your competitors, to see if they have any excess merchandise to liquidate that is something you need. A common industry sales representative may be the one to broker the deal. You know how you would feel about having cash instead of unsold goods, and your competitors surely have the same instincts. Their loss can be made into your gain.

Finally, there are a number of closeout brokers who buy inventory from sources throughout the United States, including those of distressed companies. They pay just pennies on the dollar and sell for more but still at a tremendous discount from regular pricing.

There are listings of these deals that you can find in publications as well as on the Web. Are they selling something you need?

Remember, you still have to sell or utilize the goods you purchase yourself, so don't buy anything just because it is cheap. Make sure you have a market to sell to before you make any purchases. Perhaps you should try small quantities in the beginning to see how good you will be at merchandising this type of deal. You can make a good profit, but only if you can actually turn over the goods.

Invest in Cash Instruments

Invest your excess profits in cash instruments such as certificates of deposit. This is a safe investment that will pay you interest and be fairly liquid if you should need the money. In these days of low interest rates, the returns aren't very high, and of course there is a penalty for cashing in the certificate before it is due. You can, however, invest for as few as 30 days.

You may also be able to keep your excess cash in money market funds, which will earn you interest on an ongoing basis.

If the funds you have to invest exceed $100,000, your bank will likely be able to manage your investment program for you. There is a fee for this service, but it will be offset by what you will earn if the available returns are high enough. With a sweep account, your bank will automatically transfer any excess funds (as determined by you) into your interest-bearing account and then back again to your business account when there are checks to honor. Sweeps may be made daily if needed.

You can also manage this on your own and not pay a bank fee. Start by opening an interest-bearing account and make transfers into your business account when you write checks. Once or twice a week should suffice, and you are permitted by current law to make as many transfers as you wish.

135

On the other hand, current banking regulations permit only three checks per month to be drawn on a money market account. This number will be going up over the next few years and eventually you will be able to draw one check per day. Remember, transfers are unlimited, checks are not.

Why Not Buy Your Building?

If you are looking to take out profits from your existing company and redeploy the cash somewhere else, real estate may be the way to go. Perhaps you could buy the building you already inhabit or one that has recently come on the market and you know to be a good value. Depending on your goals, you may be helping the expense side of your current company and meeting longer term goals as well.

An owner of a cash cow business must still be diligent about controlling overhead costs. Establishing a fixed cost for space by owning it is a good way to accomplish this. While taxes and utilities can go up, the mortgage payment will not. And you are acquiring equity in another asset instead of paying rent.

The amount of space you purchase may also be a consideration because if you are still in the growing stage, you will need room for expansion. However, if you are in the mature stage, you may be able to rent out any excess space, which will defray your costs even more.

The only major downside to ownership is the issue of maintenance, which will now become your responsibility. A building in need of repair could end up being a serious drain on both your financial and human resources. Take care that you fully consider the property that best suits your needs and that you have it inspected fully before purchase to make sure you are aware of the current condition. Real estate has proven to be a good value over time—lower inflation has lessened the amount of financial gain somewhat, but the value of well-maintained property seldom goes down. And your equity position will be going up.

Purchase Another Company

One of the most interesting (yet trickiest) investments of all is to purchase another company. If you know that the life span of your current business is fairly limited, you may be very wise to diversify by purchasing another company with more upside growth potential.

There is another strategy to consider as well, and that is to acquire a greater market share by purchasing one or more competing businesses. This type of consolidation often goes on in mature industries. Some companies have learned how to maximize their profits even with a low-growth scenario. If you are the one enjoying profits, acquiring higher volume without raising your overhead will drop an even greater percentage of profit to your bottom line. However, be careful about what type of deal you make. Overpaying for assets, such as equipment or a building you don't need could alter this advantage. You're in a good negotiation position. Be tough. Make sure that the two companies are a good mix.

Consider compatibility with your customer base. Have their pricing strategies been similar to yours? If you take on a company that cuts prices, some customers will expect you to cut *your* prices. If you absorb employees from another company, think about the corporate cultures. Do they have the same attitude about customer service that you do? Are their work habits and priorities compatible with yours? If there are too many differences, your entire organization may be disrupted, and your goal of higher volume at a similar or better margin could be undermined. A merger of two companies is a bit like a marriage—it can get that personal.

The question of how much to pay for a business is not as complex as it may seem. You must look at it in terms of the profits you expect from the acquisition. Once their volume is merged into yours with your overhead structure, how much profit will you see? Paying a sum equal to two to five years of that profit is a fair range, depending on your current projection for the life cycle of this business. This is also reasonable if you are acquiring assets as well. Can you cut the cost of the purchase by selling off those assets that are excess to your operation?

Another strategy to employ is to offer to the current owner a percentage of the sales volume you are able to maintain. Depending on his need to sell, you might be able to strike this kind of a deal, which would really lower your risk. There is always the risk that you will lose some customers in the transition, and this way you won't be paying for the business you can't hold. Consider what a fair commission might be and offer it. If you don't need his equipment or inventory, let the current owner liquidate them and keep the proceeds.

Make sure that you are not leveraging your own company to buy the assets of another. Excess borrowing or cash flow strains could deteriorate your current stability. Structure a deal that makes good sense.

Buying equipment, market share, new trademarks or patents, inventory, or even the services of a talented work force may enhance your existing business. But only if you buy wisely.

There are other investment alternatives beyond the four mentioned here. Some may be too sophisticated and some too risky. Remember, you are looking to enhance your profitability by putting your money to work. Stay within your level of expertise and your comfort zone.

There is another side to a mature business and it isn't so bright: margin creep.

Beware of Margin Creep

The major danger of flat growth, no growth, or merely a slight increase in revenues is that your costs will not stay the same and your margins will begin to shrink seriously. If you pay inadequate attention to tracking your monthly profit and loss statement, you can quickly find that what started as a small problem has gotten out of hand. If your company has only an acceptable level—or even a healthy level—of profitability at the moment, you must maintain or improve this profitable trend to prevent drift in the opposite direction.

When growth is flat, you must be more diligent than ever to monitor both your direct costs and your overhead expenses. If they grow without being accounted for, your profits will shrink and cash flow will become tight.

Reduce Direct Costs

Over time, the cost of the raw material that you use or the finished products that you sell is bound to go up. The increases may only be small but they will effect your operating profits. Sometimes your suppliers will give you advance notice of pricing changes, particularly if you have a supply contract, but there are also many times when your only notice will be the pricing change on the invoice itself. Someone in your organization—you or your controller—should verify all incoming invoices to make sure that price increases do not slip by, unnoticed until you see a higher expense on your profit and loss statement. There are times when you will need to absorb some of the increase, but there may also be a point when you must try to source less expensive material or pass on the cost to your customers.

Labor costs can go up as a percentage of direct costs, and the causes are less obvious, so you may not notice until your gross profit margins are seriously effected. There are several key reasons for this problem, and you want to investigate the situation and find the ones that have impacted you.

You may be overstaffed. If your sales are not growing and from time to time they are very soft, you may have too many employees. Your labor costs may be growing at a rate higher than your volume and your margins are shrinking. It is never easy to cut back staff, either by laying people off temporarily or cutting their hours, but sometimes it is absolutely necessary. If yours is a service business and sales are soft today but might be brisk tomorrow, you must be very astute about how far back you cut. If customer service deteriorates during a rush period, you could lose needed business due to customer dissatisfaction. Set labor goals and monitor them, taking action only when you are convinced it is necessary. You may be able to adjust your pricing slightly upward to account for your labor expenses.

If yours is a mature company, and the equipment and tools that you are using are equally mature, you may be up against frequent mechanical failures. Decisions must be made about replacing old equipment if this becomes too much of a problem. The cost of the excess labor needed to cope with old equipment may exceed the cost of repair or replacement. It's a judgment call, but it will help to analyze the situation by doing a cost projection.

Productivity must be constantly monitored. You must set goals and benchmarks to measure the work product of your employees. Borderline workers (those who do just enough to get by) can undermine the productivity of everyone else in the group. If your personal workload is fairly high, taking the time to hire and train replacement workers may seem overwhelming, but to not do so may create further damage that will have to be undone with even greater effort and cost. Don't settle for less than what you need.

Turn Your Attention to Overhead

Over a period of years, the cost of running any business is bound to go up as utility, phone, freight, and even postage costs increase. In a company where volume is rising, this is less of an issue because the fixed overhead expenses become a smaller percentage of the overall costs. But in mature businesses, including those that are cash cows, flat growth will not allow you to absorb higher costs without taking some action. You must monitor your own line item expenses to be alert to your cost structure. If your gross margin is 40 percent and your costs are 30 percent, your profit is only 10 percent. That's not bad if you can hold it there, but a hike in several overhead items can melt that margin away very quickly.

You should be careful about the cost of your employee benefits, especially health insurance, as this cost has continued to rise for years in excess of overall inflation. You may need to change or cut back your coverage in order to keep the cost down. It's not a popular choice to make, but one that you may be forced to confront. General business insurance coverage is another item to monitor. Compare rates year to year and be prepared to seek competitive quotes if your costs go up.

A certain amount of business entertaining is clearly a necessity— lunches to discuss future projects, dinners to add a personal touch to a business relationship, etc. And it is necessary as well to travel to see clients and suppliers, to go to trade association meetings, and to attend seminars. The ones in the Caribbean and Las Vegas are particularly informative. There is no doubt that there is an important place for your travel and entertainment as an expense item. And there is no doubt that a certain amount of it is discretionary.

When your company is vibrant and growing, this line item is less of a concern. However, if sales revenue is flat, you cannot let this category grow as a percentage of expense. And over the years, with airfares and the price of a hotel stay going up, perhaps you must cut back the amount of expense-account travel you can do. Optional expenses should not use up your needed working capital. Mature companies with limited growth potential are not courted by bankers and are seldom considered bankable. You will have to generate most of your working capital internally.

The owner's salary is another issue to address at this point, and it is probably one that should be addressed openly and honestly at various times in the life of a business. One of the interesting aspects of being in business for yourself is the ability to set your own compensation. In the 21 years I ran a company, whenever I increased my salary, I expected somebody to say something, but of course nobody ever did. This is your decision to make and you must be prudent. When your company is growing, your rewards grow along with it. Now, if revenues are flat, good sense says that your salary must also stay relatively flat. If you continue to increase it, you can cause a cash crisis. You may even have to lend money back to the business to get over short-term capital shortages. I see this salary issue a good bit in my consulting work and it makes no sense at all. You are putting your own money at risk simply to draw out more taxable dollars in salary. A large salary might gratify your ego, but it represents poor financial management.

Now that I have told you that you can't take a higher salary, I am also going to tell you that you must continue to work very hard and be more diligent now than you may have been in years. Now is the time to watch your expenditures, track them on a regular basis, and cut them wherever possible. You want to maximize the profits and put them to use where they can continue to work for you. This is a part of your business reality—understanding how to keep the company going for as long as you want and as long as it still makes financial sense. Preventive action is a good step in that direction.

Effective Turnaround Techniques

Economies go in cycles, as do entire industries and individual businesses. The steel industry in the United States is going through its third crisis in 20 years, each one making the industry a bit smaller and weaker. Those businesses that serve this sector suffer along with their customers. A decade ago, retailing was in a tailspin after leveraged buyouts. The airline industry was virtually grounded by high fuel costs. Few businesses go through their existence without hitting a wall or two. The real test is how you come off the wall.

The fact that you are in business means that you are by nature an optimist—you have very likely gone through rough times along the way and hold a strong belief that with some patience and a few minor adjustments, those times will pass. But there comes a time when the situation deteriorates to a point where action is required, and failing to take action will jeopardize the future of your entire venture. What are some of the signs that the situation may be getting out of hand? Here are six to consider:

1. Prolonged periods of no growth and diminishing profits.
2. Loss of productivity. It is taking you longer and costing you more to produce the same work.
3. Loss of a major market or customer. The industry you serve has seriously diminished or the customer whose purchases provide more than 35 percent of your business income has failed or gone out of business.
4. Loss of your capital base. You no longer have any available working capital in the business and cash flow is below what is necessary to retire obligations.
5. Changing technology and increased competition which put pressure on your current pricing structure. "New kids on the block" are forcing you to lower prices, but your existing costs are higher than theirs, meaning you can't continue a price war for the long haul.
6. Unpaid taxes, which can destroy a business in very short order. This situation should be avoided at all costs. A reasonably small amount of taxes can skyrocket to a huge amount of money with the addition of penalties and interest. And not filing a return is even more serious because this increases the amount of the possible penalties. Federal payroll tax can carry a 5 percent per month

failure-to-file penalty and a 5 percent failure-to-pay penalty for up to five months, totaling a 25 percent penalty on each indiscretion. This means that not paying your 941 withholding tax and not filing the return could cost you a 50 percent penalty. It won't take long to be buried in that debt. Sales tax is a different and in some ways more serious matter. If you have collected monies due to your state and converted them to your own use, that may be considered fraud—a criminal offense. In addition, there is a very high penalty assessed to the amount due. And as if all of this isn't enough, the enforcement options open to taxing bodies exceeds those of all other creditors. The government has the right, upon notice, to levy both your bank account and your accounts receivable. This means that your customers will be sending their money directly to the government and you will be starved of all cash. If you have begun to get into this type of trouble, red flags should be going up all over. You will receive registered letters warning of impending actions.

There may be some other problems that you have identified as very critical, even if you haven't fully faced up to them. You know the rhythm of your own business, and you know when that rhythm has been lost. The worst thing you can do is take no action. A problem won't get better on its own.

Difficult Situations Are Not Always Hopeless

You need to develop a strategy for a full scale business turnaround. Here is a four-step plan that you could use as a basic model:

1. Stabilize the operation. Troubled businesses often go spinning out of control. As a starting point you must slow yours down and get it on firmer ground.
2. Analyze the operation in great detail. Where are your strengths and how can you enhance them, and where are your weaknesses and how can you minimize or correct them?

3. Organize. Develop a recovery plan and put it on paper and in front of key individuals.
4. Institutionalize all of the changes and set benchmarks that prevent a recurrence of the problems that brought you here.

Start on Square One: Look for Stability

There comes a point in a business that has been drifting downward where it begins to slide out of control. The longer the slide, the deeper the hole, so you must take action to stabilize the business as soon as you can. Finances are the first step.

It is likely that past due money is owed to all of your vendors, perhaps to the bank, and possibly to the taxing authorities. You may be paying out money as fast as it comes in to the person who is screaming the loudest. Stop this action as it isn't getting you anywhere.

Improve your cash situation. Call everyone involved and ask for a two-week period to evaluate where you are. The calls must be made by you or a company officer. You might be surprised at how much cooperation you receive. Depending on the lateness of your payments to the bank, if you work with your bank manager, you may be able to get an interest-only payment deal for 30 or 60 days to give you breathing room. Keep a high level of communication at this point. If you have already gone into the workout department, this will not be possible. Workout departments are setup to liquidate loans, not renegotiate them. If your tax situation hasn't gotten into the levy stage, call the taxing body and set up an appointment. That will buy some time. As for your vendors, they may be threatening all manner of actions, but you probably have learned from your own collection activity that forced collection of an unsecured debt (which includes virtually all vendor credit) is not an easy task. There are a number of court proceedings to go through first and that can take months. You don't like to hear the threats, but they have little teeth.

Next, you must quickly bring in as much cash as you can. You must make sure that your own collection activity is pursued very aggressively. Unless your margins have been razor thin, offer a small discount incentive for payment. The same deal may be offered for new projects—a discount for an upfront deposit or quick payment terms. You need as much cash as you can pull together, and your outgoing payment moratorium along with active collections should help.

Now your cash effort will be directed at liquidating any excess inventory or equipment. Take care that you are getting rid of only the excess merchandise. In a panic, some companies dump usable goods to raise cash, but in the long run that only magnifies its losses. Try an in-house sale to maximize return or use a broker if you need to. Remember that all sales below regular markup will affect your profit picture; you need the cash *now* so it is worth it. Just don't be surprised when your profit and loss statement looks pretty poor. Another point to consider is that if you have an outstanding bank loan, your equipment is likely part of the security for the loan. If what you are selling has been fully depreciated, you can go ahead and sell it, but if not, you may need the permission of the bank. Minor machinery doesn't count here.

Form a support team.   The job ahead is a very big one and you will need the help of others to accomplish it. Now is the time to put a working team into place. Hopefully there are some key employees who are loyal and talented and can be counted on when the going gets tough. You will also need a few outside professionals, including your attorney and accountant. If you don't already have a good business attorney, choose one carefully. You need experience here. Schedule a meeting with as many of these folks as you can bring together, and have an open, honest exchange about the current situation. You need ideas and help. You won't get it if you don't ask for it, or if you're not honest about your situation.

Pull back from unfinished projects.   You may have begun a variety of new projects such as product development or marketing programs as an attempt at reenergizing your company. In your panic to "do something," you may not have been as thoughtful as you should have been. Call at least a temporary halt to these activities so that you can review them at a calmer time and perhaps allow your support team to consider your plans. You need feedback from others, and now is the time to ask for it. Conserve your capital and your human resources as well.

Cut all unnecessary expense. If there is any obvious overspending in your direct expense, now is the time to take action. The likely excess expense is for labor and the reason may be that you have been reluctant to lay off employees. Now you must get serious and do whatever needs to be done. If you don't have productive work for someone, she is costing you money that you don't have. You must correct this as soon as possible.

Everyone else is also subject to a cost review, including you. Can you afford a temporary cut in pay? Can you forgo some of your perks? Tough times require tough measures. If you have some long-time employees who have done well and shared in the success, see if they are also willing to share the sacrifice. Chances are that they care, and depending on their personal circumstances, you may be pleasantly surprised at the loyalty of the people around you. In a ten-year consulting career, I have seen more cooperation than resistance, but cooperation happens primarily when everyone feels that efforts are in place to turn things around. Your communication and leadership skills are critical here.

Communicate in a way that promotes stability. A business developing some serious problems is not doing so unnoticed. Your employees likely know because inventory or supplies are decreasing or sales have been exceptionally low. There is always talk in the work environment and word gets around very quickly. Now is the time for you to communicate with all of your stakeholders. You have already spoken with creditors (be sure you keep up the dialogue—they get more nervous when they get no response than when they get bad news). Your employees need some official word, giving them a sense that there is leadership in place and action is being taken to turn things around. You want to keep good employees in place. They will in turn communicate a more positive attitude to the public, which may include your customers. This is particularly important if your current problems have had some negative results, such as poor delivery, inadequate supplies or inventory, or deteriorating customer service.

Square Two: Analyze Your Operation

At this point, the business should be standing on firmer ground. You have some breathing room, but not much. You and your team must conduct an in-depth analysis of your entire operation as soon as possible in order to determine where corrective actions must be taken. While some businesses are underperforming on all levels, most have one primary deficiency that has manifested itself in one of three areas.

1. Sales volume has dropped with no other cost adjustments. The breakeven point is not being met by current revenue.
2. The gross profit margin has decreased and operating profits are insufficient to meet overhead expenses.
3. Overhead costs are not being monitored and they have escalated, raising the breakeven point beyond current sales levels.

A closer look at sales. Start first with comparisons year to year and period to period (for example, third quarter 1998 against third quarter 1999) to track when and in what areas your volume has dropped. Look at unit sales as well as dollar sales to determine where volume has flattened, gone down, or even increased. Chances are that there has been growth in at least some areas, and that is where you need to focus your attention now. Are you maximizing sales of *all* items from your current product list? Be realistic in your review: if growth isn't likely, you will have to focus your attention on costs. If you can revitalize some areas of revenue, you must determine how much capital you will need to execute a turnaround and how you will find it.

Are gross profits on the way down? Making your breakeven point and getting back into the black involves gross profit as well as total volume. Have your direct costs gone up, lowering your gross profit? If so, why? Are the costs or increases resulting from inefficiencies or from unavoidable increases, such as a rise in utility rates? Can increased costs be passed on to buyers?

Check for overhead creep. Once again, you want to look over every line item of overhead. Has something increased as a percentage of sales because revenue is down? Or have you let some items grow without controls? Has insurance cost increased but you haven't looked at your coverage or gotten new quotes? If you must lower your breakeven, cuts in overhead are critical, and no area can be spared. Use a knife, not a hatchet; you want to cut fat, not muscle.

Now analyze the rest. The last three items for review represent the final steps in the Square Two, analysis, phase. Consider the following three issues:

1. Debt service. Are you being choked by loan payments that are too steep? Does it appear as if payback of past-due vendor credit will dry up all of your cash flow? If this is the problem area, tough negotiations and solutions will have to be tried, which will be reviewed in the next phase.
2. Is there still a market? Has your business gone beyond its prime? Is it possible that regardless of what you do, there is little new business or business growth to be had? Is there enough market left for you to restructure a smaller, more efficient company? Do you have the financial resources to enter a new market—the capital you will need to create, fund, and sell new products or services?
3. Are you enthusiastic enough to accomplish the task? A business turnaround is hard and time-consuming work. It requires commitment, a generous amount of creativity, substantial energy, and a sense of optimism. Ask yourself if you really have the stamina to put the effort into the job ahead. You must have a burning desire to see this through

because chances are, you will be working harder for less money, at least for a while. If you clearly aren't enthusiastic enough to achieve a turnaround, perhaps it is time for you to consider an exit strategy. Turn over the reins to a successor, sell out, or close up. Don't start the process only to give up too soon. If you aren't totally convinced you want to face the challenge yourself, the sooner you find a way out, the better you will be able to protect yourself.

Square Three: A Recovery Strategy

Once you know where the problem areas are, you must create a strategic plan to correct the problems. There are too many specific areas that an individual company must look at to detail them all in a single chapter. Following are *some* of the highlights to consider.

Reducing debt. You may be able to reduce debt service. Minor debt restructure is not very difficult, and even a major rewrite of leases and loans is possible in order to improve the cash flow of the company. Remember that your creditors would rather get slow payment than no payment.

You must first know exactly how much money you will have on a monthly basis in order to retire current debt. Once you have made arrangements with creditors, you *must* live up to your agreements. You will find that there is little patience left if you don't.

You must prioritize your debt and handle the most critical claims first. Those creditors who are in a position to take action against you must be dealt with first.

If you can't get all creditors to agree, you always have the option of filing for Chapter 11 bankruptcy reorganization, which will force a plan that all creditors will have to follow. We will cover this at greater length later in this chapter.

Taxing bodies have the power to levy (seize) your accounts if you haven't met obligations. However, serious negotiation with the collection department will usually get you up to 24 months to pay back arrearages. If you are able to make an up-front payment, that should seal the deal. Revenue agents are motivated by instant recovery.

Your bank has a secured position on your assets, including your bank account. You can negotiate if your loan hasn't gotten too delinquent and been moved to the workout department, which is actually a collections department. The bankers in that department are less likely to deal; their only interest is liquidation, not the continuation of your business. Rescheduling principal payments is possible, and in some circumstances a complete restructuring of your loan can be done.

A landlord has the right to evict you from his building and perhaps even lock you out while your possessions are inside. Try to restructure your lease, spreading out any delinquencies over a period of time and keeping current payment current. Most landlords don't want to go through the time and expense of eviction—give yours a reason not to do it. He will lose less money keeping you as a tenant if you make a serious attempt at paying your obligation. Show you are trying, and chances are you can stay for the present.

Perhaps you have too much space. Ask if you would be permitted to vacate some of the excess or sublet some to help out with the rent. Are there products or services you could barter with your landlord that would reduce your back obligation or even lower the current rent? Communicate and be creative—a good plan may easily be accepted.

Unsecured or vendor creditors may be the most annoying of the group, but in reality, they are the least dangerous. You are probably under a barrage of phone calls that are both demeaning and very stressful. And you may be having trouble getting supplies. There are a number of strategies to try.

First, you should try to take the calls and explain your situation, asking for some understanding and indulgence. You may be able to work out a deal with some of your suppliers. Perhaps you can offer a long-term payout of the past-due amount and at the same time do current business on a current-payment basis. A deal like this could be a win for you both. You continue to have valued vendors, and they get paid off while keeping a customer. You may be required to go on C.O.D. and pay some if the old debt down before normal credit relations are restored.

Unfortunately, not all companies are patient or astute. Some will escalate their collection calls into verbal abuse. If this happens, cease all communication and refer them to your attorney. There is nothing to save here and no reason to engage.

In reality, their options are fairly limited. They can take you through the legal process, which will take time, and you always have the right of appeal. Depending on whether you are in small claims or full court, a good attorney can hold off a collection action for up to a year. Depending on what your assets are and whether they are already pledged as security, there may not even be much to attach to satisfy a judgment. Do remember that your bank account can be attached and funds confiscated to satisfy a claim.

This doesn't mean that you are trying to avoid your responsibilities or that you should want to avoid the obligations of your company. Of course you wish you weren't in your current situation. But you can't create capital where there is none. You must keep your eye on the goal, which is to reinvigorate your business so that the cash flow is once again good enough to meet all obligations. Don't let creditors distract you from this goal. And by all means, don't overpromise. Determine how much available cash you will have, and try to satisfy as many people as you can with that money.

Marketing. Accentuate the positive aspects of your company—you need to get back to the business of business instead of disaster control. Your analysis of your sales may have shown you some areas that have potential for growth. You must explore and exploit these possibilities, because in order to move forward, you will need to maintain the sales you currently have as well as find new sources of revenue. Can you enlarge the geographical area you serve? Can you do more business with your existing customers by selling them additional products or services? Can you diversify and move into associated markets?

While your business situation has been deteriorating, it is unlikely that you have done much marketing or spent as much time in sales as you have needed to. It is hard to put on the sparkling sales personality when all you see around you is crisis. By this time, you should have become stable enough to be positive with new prospects and to capture them with your enthusiasm.

Marketing material, as well as a marketing plan, are important here. You don't have to throw big dollars at your prospects, but you do have to invest time and your own creativity. Your "turn-around team" may be of some help here. If they are outsiders, ask for their opinion of how you look for potential customers.

Budgeting. Create a budget and use it! You read about them in "how to" books and learn about them in business classes, but actually taking the time to make one is something most small business owners fail to do. There are so many other tasks that are pressing and this is one that is put on the back burner. But now that you have gone through some tough financial times, surely you can see the value of establishing financial controls and using them with discipline.

You begin with a line item document created either annually or quarterly. Unless there are some clear and compelling reasons to use one, a monthly budget will be unnecessarily confusing. Expenses tend to come in bunches. One month may be particularly light and in the next you are hit with the full amount. Consider your phone bills—long distance charges often appear on a delayed basis. If you work on a monthly budget, some months may look so bad you will panic, and the next ones so good, you will think you're on your way to easy street. The truth is somewhere in the middle.

On the income side, this is true as well. Your sales are unlikely to stay the same month after month. Consider your past history and your future plans and set quarterly goals that reflect these expectations.

You know what kinds of profit margins you will need; plan for them. Then review your actual progress against those goals. If you haven't met them, the time to take action is immediate. One bad quarter won't destroy a business, but when insufficient profits go into a second and a third quarter without any corrections, you're back behind the eight ball again.

Rewriting your business plan. Rewrite your business plan for the new, improved, and reinvigorated company. This is the document that incorporates all of what you now know about the operation of the business, plus the changes you have made, and sets goals for the next few years to keep you stable and on the road to full financial recovery.

Square Four: Develop and Maintain a Long-Term Strategy

Once a business is back on its feet and has regained some of its previous vitality, the time has come to put into place a long-term plan that will continue its forward momentum. There are several elements to implement, and you may wish to add some of your own to the ones I suggest here. These are ways to further ensure that you will know where you wish to go—which makes it more likely that you will get there.

Keep up with your advisory board. Being in business for yourself can be a very isolating position. Perhaps when you began experiencing problems, you looked around for a good source of advice and didn't find any that was easily accessible. If you put together the suggested "turnaround team" and it worked, why not keep it up? Even if you never quite found the right group, keep trying. There is a good reason that companies have outside boards and you should follow that model. It allows you to bounce new ideas off of other people, and ask for advice when you can't come up with solutions. Schedule quarterly meetings and create and keep an agenda that covers all of your current issues. You may get some new ideas and a fresh perspective, and just talking through your own concerns may help. Use outsiders who are interested and have something to contribute. Pay a small director's fee ($300 perhaps) and keep your relationship professional.

Increase your level of organization. If you have never had an organizational chart, now is the time to create one. You may not have quite learned how to delegate authority in the past—often an entrepreneurial weakness. Then you had to exercise strong centralized control to steer the company through tough waters. But your business will be better off if you give up some of this control to other key people. Encourage independent decision making and support others' work; they will be more productive.

Here are three techniques you can use to assist and educate everyone in your company to move to a new, flatter and more decentralized, model of management.

1. Create formal job descriptions. Each manager should know what her area of responsibility is and what level of outcome is expected. Those who control costs should be responsible for meeting their budgetary goals.

2. Put up an organizational chart for everyone to see. Have subordinates report to managers and managers report to you. Don't get involved in day-to-day situations that go outside the chain of command.

3. Allow managers and department heads to have a level of budgetary control. This may be accomplished by seeking their input on the overall budget or by giving them a discretionary budget of their own. Make them a part of the financial team and allow them to see the results of their efforts. When the financial circumstances permit, bonuses for meeting or exceeding goals is a great idea.

Set annual benchmark numbers. Review performance against your benchmarks. At the end of each year, your inside team should set goals of revenues and profitability for the upcoming year. On a quarterly basis, you want to review your progress against those goals. The team then decides whether to modify the goals or make changes to existing operations in order to meet them.

Determine an exit strategy. There is much to learn from a business turnaround. You have likely gotten deeper inside the workings of your business than perhaps you ever had before. You have been forced to reexamine your enthusiasm and commitment. And you possibly gave at least brief consideration to walking away. Perhaps you gave it substantial thought.

Perhaps you have realized that some day you will have to make the move away from the company, and the sooner you determine when or how you will do that, the better the situation you can create for yourself. Perhaps you have a family member in place and you are contemplating succession. You must train him and then determine what financial arrangement you can make to transfer ownership or management.

Would you be able to sell to an insider? Has someone already been identified as the leading candidate? What deals are possible and how soon can you begin to work on it?

You may need to consider an outside individual or company. You need to prepare your business to be presented at its best advantage—a process that could take up to three years. Then you must decide who will handle the legalities, how much you can ask for the business, and how to conduct negotiations. This is a complicated and time-consuming process, and preparation is the key to success.

You don't want to find yourself in the position of wanting or needing to dispose of the company in a rush—you won't be able to make a good deal from that position. Remember, you had a plan to get into business, and you made a plan to stay in business; isn't it logical to have a plan to exit business?

Plan B: Chapter 11 Reorganization

Suppose you have taken all or most of the steps recommended and you still haven't come to resolution with creditors. Their pressure and demands are keeping you from taking action needed to improve the performance of your business. Or you have analyzed your current and future cash flow positions and realize that you won't be able to pay everyone back in full. All is not lost. You still have a legal remedy that will help you to save your ongoing company. You can file for protection under Chapter 11 of the Federal Bankruptcy Code. This will hold off your creditors until you can propose a plan for paying them back at least part of your indebtedness.

Years ago, a bankruptcy signified the end of the life of a business. Not true now. Airlines such as Continental and TWA are still flying, stores like Macy's and Bloomingdale's are still selling, and companies like Wheeling-Pittsburgh Steel are still manufacturing. Thousands of smaller companies are still operating after a successful Chapter 11.

You should learn as much as you can about the bankruptcy process and pick an attorney who is both knowledgeable about it and has a successful track record. This is not the place for rookies.

What the Process Looks Like

Once a petition is filed, the court issues what is called an automatic stay, which stops all creditor actions including tax levies and even sheriff's sales. You then have an exclusive period of 120 days to propose a plan through the court to your creditors stating how much and how soon you expect to pay them back.

A typical case takes from six months to one year between the filing and the confirmation of a plan. There are some costs to bear here. The highest will be your attorney, who may charge a retainer of from $5,000 to $15,000 and run up total fees of double that amount. An accountant will be needed to file monthly reports with the courts, and the U.S. trustee will bill you for fees based on the total volume of your business. This charge will average several thousand dollars per quarter. You will be required to keep all current taxes paid and returns filed on time. All of the past-due taxes will be paid under the plan.

Under a bankruptcy proceeding, your debt is categorized under four general headings and each category will be handled in a slightly different way. With the exception of administrative debt, you will have up to 72 months to pay back all of the monies that are due. The debt categories and criteria for payment are as follows:

- *Administrative debt.* This is all debt incurred after the filing, such as legal and professional fees and any vendor credit. If the company owed wages at the time of the filing, claims not to exceed $2,500 per individual will also be in this category. All wage claims in excess of that amount will be unsecured. Any post-petition tax debt comes under this category as well, although it is not a good idea to incur any.

  Administrative debt will be paid upon confirmation of the plan by a prior agreement with the creditor. Ongoing trade debt will be paid as due, and sometimes professionals such as lawyers and accountants will agree to payouts over a period of time.
- *Secured debt.* This is all types of lending, including bank loans, car loans, and equipment loans that are secured to collateral, assuming the value of the collateral exceeds the debt. Any portion of the debt that does not have sufficient collateral becomes unsecured. For example, a car loan has a balance of $10,000 due and the car is only worth $5,000. Five thousand dollars of the loan is secured and the balance is unsecured.

Any debts that have been litigated through to a judgment will be secured if there is collateral to secure the amount. A judgment where there are no assets is worthless.

Secured debt is paid in full according to the terms negotiated by creditors and debtors.

- *Priority unsecured debt.* The debt owing to taxing bodies comes under this heading. The principal of the tax due as well as any interest that is due belongs here. Penalties assessed to the taxes, if they have not been liened and secured, fall to the next category. This debt must be paid back over a period of up to 72 months, along with any statutory interest.

- *Unsecured debt.* This is most vendor debt, any of the previously identified secured debt that is undercollateralized, and any tax penalties that have not been previously liened. A portion of this debt—often in the range of 25–40 percent—is paid back over 72 months, along with interest.

During the course of the allowable 120 days, you will operate the business as the "debtor in possession." The court is protecting you from your creditors and it is also overseeing the use of your assets so that they can be used to satisfy your creditors. At some point you will file two documents, a disclosure statement and the plan of reorganization.

The disclosure statement is meant to give the court, and primarily your creditors, a reading of your current financial circumstances. You will list all of your debts—the past ones and any new ones incurred since the filing, such as the legal and accounting fees and any outstanding vendor credit. You will include future financial projections to show that you will be able to fulfill the plan you are proposing.

One of the most important features of the disclosure statement is known as the liquidation analysis. You must analyze for your creditors what the company would be worth if it went into total liquidation versus its value as an operating company. The point is to prove that they will receive more of a return if you continue as a going concern. Once you add up all the fees and costs involved in most liquidations, it is usually in everyone's interest to have you continue in business, aside from your desire to do so. And this is the basis of the law as well. The courts are charged with securing the highest return for creditors, and everyone understands that this usually comes from a company that is back on its feet.

The plan will show how each creditor has been classified and how each will be treated (paid) under the plan.

If your company has accumulated a good bit of debt, here is one way to be able to continue operation and get another shot at correcting any past mistakes. Most creditors will benefit from your hard work.

One of the most frequently asked questions is whether companies will do business—buy or sell—with a company in bankruptcy. The answer is a resounding yes. People are more used to it now and see businesses all the time that file under bankruptcy protection and go on. It is even possible to get credit again. Banks may lend to a company in Chapter 11 with court permission.

It isn't easy to go through a Chapter 11, starting with the decision to file. But there are times when it is the only decision to be made. You will learn a great deal from the experience and, no doubt, learn how not to make the same mistakes again. You will also become a lot stronger and a lot more resilient.

Protect Yourself from Contingent Liability

One of the primary reasons to incorporate a new business is to protect the individual owners from personal liability for corporate debts. But along the way, a number of exceptional situations may arise that alter that protection, and while you may not be in a position to change many of them, you should be aware and try to maintain the corporate shield as much as possible. The four exceptions are as follows:

1. All taxes that are trust fund (employment taxes such as withheld federal, state, and local tax) and collected tax (such as sales tax) remain the liability of the individual responsible for collecting and remitting such taxes. Many taxing bodies can be relentless in their pursuit of delinquent tax monies.

2. Any bank loans on which you have signed a personal guarantee may carry personal liability. Over the past few years, most bankers have stopped insisting that the spouse also sign a guarantee. This is an acknowledgment that many two-earner families keep individual finances separate. Your bank may be the exception and may require two signatures, in which case you may need to find a new bank.

   If both parties are not signators, then any property owned jointly by them cannot be confiscated for nonpayment by one party of a loan. This is how you protect your home.

3. If you have signed personal guarantees on any vendor credit applications, then they may take action against you individually. When signing credit applications, do so *only* as a corporate officer. Read before you sign your name, and use your title to signify that you are acting in an official capacity.

   If a vendor insists that you sign the personal guarantee, you need to decide what is more important, getting credit or staying protected. Perhaps you can take more time to develop a track record with the vendor and then ask for credit without the signature. Most companies want the business and will relent after a while.

4. Any fraud committed by a company can be charged to the owner personally. Fraud may involve taking payments under false pretense or purposely not delivering the type or quantity of goods ordered. A trial could result in the owner being held liable.

Most of these situations are ones that you don't expect to experience in your business career. But it is important to understand how much your business finances can be attached to your personal finances.

If you are still nervous about the risk, there is something else you can do to insulate yourself from corporate obligations. Should you have any liability for unpaid debts, only assets that are in your name alone can be attached. Jointly-owned property is safe from claims on you as an individual. Discuss your situation thoroughly with your attorney to see how you can best protect yourself. Last minute property transfers will usually *not* work as they will be seen by the court as an attempt to defraud creditors.

You are in business to earn a living and provide economic opportunity for others. It is likely you've worked hard to get where you are, even if you are presently is in a difficult situation. If you wanted easy answers, independent business provides very few of them. You had the courage to get into the game, and often it takes courage to stay. Understand your circumstances, put together a strong team, and develop a good strategic plan. Then use the creativity and energy you still have to get a fresh start.

CASE STUDY: J.E.'s Breakeven Point

By year three, Jack felt that he had an excellent sense of what it took to operate his company efficiently. The staff and overhead cost that he had budgeted for year three had been well thought out and appeared reasonable. Operating costs of $870,000 were used to determine breakeven volume.

At a 23 percent gross profit margin, sales of $3.7 million generated operating profits of $860,000, which was the breakeven target. With current sales of almost $1 million over this number, J.E.'s financial health was solid.

The next few years were spent working on enlarging the customer base, but resulted in little actual growth—new business was mostly replacing old business that was lost.

The Mature Company

For four years, J.E. seemed to run very efficiently. Sales volume was slightly under $5 million, cash flow was positive, and everyone seemed satisfied—including the bank that had its first loan retired in a timely manner. However, overhead costs were going up, with everyone costing "just a bit" more. The salespeople now had cars, Jack's draw had gone to $180,000 annually, and some of his personal expenses were covered by the company.

Overhead had increased by $100,000, although this had not reflected totally on net (before tax) profits. The difference was made up by a slightly higher gross margin created by better purchasing skills.

The company seemed on solid footing until a massive change in market conditions in the mid-1980s.

A serious recession in the Midwestern industrial market caused sales to drop dramatically over a six-month period, with many of the losses permanent as customers shuttered parts of their operations. At the end of the slide, sales were off by 30 percent and now registered annually at $3.5 million. With overhead now at $970,000, the outcomes were substantially changed:

Sales	$3,500,000	
Cost of goods	2,695,000	77%
Gross profit	805,000	
Less overhead	970,000	
Profit (loss)	$ (165,000)	

This eight-year-old company was in a serious struggle for survival. The major focus became cost cutting and a strict budgeting process. Everyone realized that the breakeven point had to be lowered to below $800,000 in order to reduce the losses at the lower current volume. It is also possible to raise margins in some companies by lowering direct costs, but this was not an option for J.E. because its material costs were as low as they could be. In fact, because costs were tied to volume buying, it was difficult to keep them from rising as volume dropped. Much of the working capital had dried up in funding the losses. The bank let J.E. draw down the full amount of its line of credit, but would not entertain any new financing until the situation changed. Tight inventory management was crucial to this process.

Making a Transition

In 1991, J.E. Industrial Distributing made a very critical decision for its future. Three years of aggressive selling effort had resulted in less than $1 million of new sales. Profits were back, but they remained small. More volume was the only answer.

Another specialty distribution company whose sales had also dropped in the mid-1980s and not come back was facing the same problem. Its sales seemed stuck at $5.5 million. The two companies merged.

The results were quick and dramatic. The consolidation cut overhead for each company by almost 40 percent—office and warehouse space was shared, as was administrative staff. Two trucks were all they needed together, and one salesperson was cut. The combined volume of $9 million was achieved with surprisingly low overhead and resulted in before-tax profits of almost 6 percent. Growth to this day has remained slow but steady, and the partnership has been a win for both companies.

Discussion Questions

1. What budgetary controls should be in place to prevent increases in overhead?

2. How should a company diversify to prevent or at least minimize the effects of a downturn?

3. How much working capital is necessary to protect the business?

4. What economies are found in consolidation and mergers?

7

Planning Your Exit Strategy

Take the Money and Run

You can't always get what you want . . . but if you try sometime, you just might find, you get what you need.

   —The Rolling Stones

Learning Objectives

Once you have completed this chapter, you will be able to:

✔ Describe the dynamics of a family business and understand what characterizes the successful ones.

✔ Create an exit strategy that meets the management needs of the business and the financial needs of the owner.

✔ Understand the value of a business as a going concern and how to position a company for sale at the highest price.

✔ Describe various financial options involved in the sale of a business and analyze which is most beneficial.

When you go into business, it is difficult to plan for anything longer than short range and nearly impossible to plan beyond five years out. There is so much to learn and so much to accomplish in the here and now. And once you get into the day-to-day work, it gets absorbing. This may have been your lifelong dream and you may expect to make it a permanent career. But some business owners see their company in terms of an investment and their goal is to build up the value and then cash it in.

Whatever your goal, the reality is that your business will likely be the primary equity that you will rely on as a source of funds for retirement. You must plan on how you will eventually liquidate this equity. Or you may want to plan how you will keep it intact if something happens to you. Or perhaps how you might pass it on.

Ask yourself honestly if the company could survive—much less thrive—without your leadership. If the answer is no, or you have strong doubts, you must address this issue. If there are potential successors inside the company for ownership or leadership, you must identify them and begin to give them the tools to fill in for you if needed. Beyond the operational expertise and the selling insights, you must also provide them with full financial disclosure. It is never good policy to be the only one to understand the inside financial workings of your business. You operate with the full picture of the business, inside and out. Shouldn't another key individual have that total picture as well?

In addition, if you are in a stable cash position, it would be prudent to buy a large term life insurance policy that the company pays for, owns, and is the beneficiary of. Should anything happen to you, this extra capital would allow for a smoother transition and help to protect assets for your family. Buying a policy when you are young is a wise move because that will keep down the cost.

The Heir Apparent—Family Succession

Of the millions of small businesses in this country, a large number of them employ more than one member of the family. It may start on a part-time basis: wife helping out husband or children working summers or weekends. Eventually, for many, this becomes a full-time involvement and the business becomes officially a family business. The problem here is that succession is just assumed and not planned for, and it seldom works well without a plan. And a sense of humor helps as well.

The pitfalls here are many, starting with the reality that it is difficult to forge out and rule as the "crown prince" or "crown princess." The frustration that comes with this ill-defined job is such that many offspring leave the company or stop taking interest and never get fully prepared to step into the leadership position. And the day comes when they must do so. The transition is usually not very successful. There is a reason that only one in three family businesses pass successfully to the second generation and only one in eight pass on to the third.

The failure of succession can be a very tragic scenario and is one to be avoided at all costs. Aside from the evident financial implications, namely the loss of family assets, the human implications are quite painful as well. There is a profound sense of failure that can be seen in business owners' offspring who are struggling to keep the company afloat. They feel a great amount of pressure to succeed. If they are ill-prepared or the company has passed its prime, they won't give up easily and often preside over a weak company far too long, until there is nothing to salvage. The business just folds with no return to anyone and perhaps creates personal debt as well.

The Business Must Be Prepared as Well as the Successors

A company cannot just fall into the hands of a successor. It must be prepared by making sure that the resources to continue it, primarily financial, are available. If you have used a substantial portion of the company's cash flow to fund your lifestyle instead of building equity, then there will be less to pass on. It is totally your decision on how to allocate funds. Just don't be surprised when the company is simply too fragile for any type of succession, family or otherwise. A business should be exceptionally financially secure before it is passed on to a new generation.

New leaders will not have your level of expertise. You had the vision and you understood it better than anyone else; your offspring may not. You developed a group of outside associates over the years to rely on for business advice or resources. They may not be available to your offspring. And banks may be less likely to extend financing to unproved leaders. So if there is no cash cushion to smooth the way through the early mistakes and the need for growth, how can you begin to expect a smooth transition? And if there is some payout to you involved, that will only make the situation more difficult. You have a stake in this scenario, both as a caring parent and an investor. Be wise about the decisions and prudent about the financing.

Are the Drive and the Desire There?

Ask yourself, "Do my offspring have the necessary tools?" It may be a matter of style or talent or just a matter of some learning, but this is a question to be answered candidly. You know what the company needs and you know what you're working with. Is it a good match? If you have any doubts, try to have an open dialogue about it. You may find out whether you are dealing with young people who do feel driven to take over, or ones who feel merely obligated to do so.

Perhaps you can liberate both of you at the same time. You might be able to sell out to another individual or company, and your offspring might be able to stay on in a sales or managerial capacity, if all parties are comfortable with the arrangement. You could work out an employment contract that would allow for a smooth transition and future opportunity for your offspring. Even if you all cash out and leave, a good severance package will be valuable in assisting in career change. You may well learn that you have had reluctant successors all along.

I had a customer from one family business that was operated by the second and third generation until they made the decision to sell out, a decision forced by deteriorating business conditions. The grandson went on to pursue a career as a photographer at the age of 36, which he admitted was what he had wanted all along. My own third generation succession began suddenly, and although I had run the family company for more than 20 years, my writing career had to be put on hold until I planned my own exit. I valued the experience, even if it wasn't necessarily acquired by choice.

Meeting Your Own Financial Needs

The next question to ask is how this transition can meet your financial requirements. Do you need to get all or most of your equity out of the business? If the answer is yes, then you are looking at selling off the company even if it is to a member of the family. Can you get enough financing from the business's assets to be paid out a substantial portion upfront? It is very tricky to finance a member of your own family. It would be far better for the bank to hold the paper than for you to act as banker.

If, down the road, any forbearance is required when times get tough, it is a personal thing between parent and child, not strictly a business deal between banker and customer. Any sort of long-term payout—for either the purchase price, or a consulting/employment contract—is at risk whether the buyer is a family member or a stranger. This risk is increased with family because difficulty in meeting obligations becomes personal.

Make the Deal Official and Legal

Structuring an informal deal for the transition of your business to a family member is not a prudent thing to do. Perhaps you think you can just retire and be kept on the payroll. Or perhaps you haven't thought it through at all.

Whatever you decide, it should be put in writing with the aid of a good attorney and a good accountant. There are legal as well as tax implications to consider.

For example, ownership must be clear in order for any outside financing to be done. Once you are no longer the active manager, do you want to continue to be liable for any bank loans? There are personal liabilities to taxing authorities as well, and responsibilities for legal proceedings. Don't you want to extract yourself from these obligations? Why should you be liable for decisions made by someone else?

You must pay personal taxes on what you draw or what you receive from your company. Are you still getting a fully taxable paycheck? Is what you are getting a purchase of your equity? Is there a capital gains tax to pay? What is the dollar amount of the gain? Are you eligible for Social Security?

These questions need to be answered and the deal needs to be clarified in writing, providing the most favorable terms for each of you. Along the way, you may have had a very casual business relationship with your offspring. Even if it has worked well, when it comes to the financial terms of this deal, you need to be more formal. It will protect you both. And it will protect your relationship down the road. Each person has the right to accept or reject the contract as written.

Preparing for a Sale

If you are selling to a successor or an insider, there is little reason to take a few years and get the company ready to be sold for the best available price. She will already know both the strengths and the weaknesses, and the time and money involved in the preparation are not justified. But if your sale is to an outsider, you will need the time and the knowledge to get the best deal possible.

You must understand how to value your company first, in order to know how to increase that value. You know that your balance sheet shows the equity or book value of your assets, but this is seldom the figure you rely on when looking to sell the business. First of all, your assets may be worth more than the amount listed on the books particularly if you have used accelerated depreciation in order to save on taxes. And most importantly, your balance sheet will not reflect the value of your intangible assets: your name, your customer list, the goodwill you have in the market, and even your expertise. The value of these items really comes into play when you sell the business. Their real value is with a going concern.

You set your price based on two criteria: (1) the value of your assets and (2) the return on investment (profitability). The typical buyer will value the return based on the level of the risk. The lower the risk, the higher the return on your earnings and the higher the selling price. Conversely, the higher the risk, the lower the price.

The earnings on which you will base your sale price will be the average earnings for the past three years. Even if you have used the business to fund your lifestyle, you will have a chance to restate the earnings, adding back in what is commonly known as "owner's excess draw." Added to this price may be the value of the liquid assets, which include cash, inventory, and accounts receivable. This number will also be adjusted by any unusable inventory or uncollectible receivables (those over 60 or 90 days old may be put in that category). You will retain the right to collect those accounts, if possible.

The range of return that an outside buyer expects is based on the current rate of the safest investments, which in 1999 is around 6 percent. A business investment would start at double that number or 12 percent and go as high as 30 percent. This means that a company earning $12,000 net profit would be worth a high of $100,000 ($12,000 is 12 percent of $100,000) and a low of $40,000 ($12,000 is 30 percent of $40,000). So it makes sense to lower the risk to reach the highest return.

Four of the considered risk factors when buying a company are:

1. *The earnings record.* How steady has it been and over how long a period? If the past three years were erratic, the risk will seem high. If each period yielded the same amount of money, the company would be worth more. When doing your long-term preparation, you could always defer some income or expense from one year to the next to smooth out the earnings. The profits remain the same, only they are allocated differently.

2. *The age of the company.* If it is too young, a buyer may say it has no solid track record. If it is too old, the buyer may believe it to be past its prime. If yours is a mature company, you will need to put together a package showing how it has changed and grown over the years and how it is currently positioned to meet challenges and to continue into a vibrant long-term future.

3. *The current market prospects for the product or service.* Is your market stagnant? If it is growing, at what rate? If there is any statistical material describing growth in the particular market segment you serve, make sure you include the data that you give to a potential buyer.

4. *The type and value of your tangible assets.* A manufacturing business with substantial equipment that could be sold off to raise capital is viewed as a lower risk. A service com-

pany with primarily intangible assets is seen as a higher risk because there is little solid collateral.

A range of return between 12 and 30 percent can be a very substantial difference—earnings of $100,000 would bring a price range for the company from $300,000 to $800,000. Making changes *before* you sell the company is very worthwhile.

Adjustments to Earnings

The earnings reflected on your profit and loss statement will be adjusted in both directions to account for any known future changes or extraordinary items.

Your earnings will be *reduced* for the following reasons:

- Known increases in rent or other expenses such as insurance, etc.
- Needed imminent replacement of equipment or vehicles. You may have deferred this expense—new owners will know they cannot.
- If economic hard times have forced you to take a salary below what your job is worth, the difference will be discounted here.
- A mature company that has not changed its products or marketing will be discounted to account for the cost to develop new markets.

Your earnings will be *increased* for the following reasons:

- If owner's salary is in excess of the going rate for a similar manager, the difference will be added here.
- Excess benefits for the owner or his family for insurance, club benefits, tickets to sporting events, etc.
- Auto expenses not absolutely necessary for the company. Even if the car is titled to the business, private use is nei-

ther technically expensable nor a tax deduction; it is a ben-
efit for the owner.
- Any wages paid to family members for nonessential work.
- Excess travel and entertainment.
- Additional expenses associated with current management
that will not continue.

You can make a list of these items and review them for yourself to
see how much impact they have had on your earnings. Then you
will disclose them to a potential buyer, who will not be surprised—these items are expected. However, if you are preparing
in advance to sell the business, why not discontinue some or even
most of these costs so that the profits drop now to your bottom
line. A correct financial statement is easier to use than a restated
one. And a new owner looking to finance the purchase will have
an easier time getting a bank loan based on *actual* earnings.

Is it worth making these changes? Considering that you can
receive as much as eight times your earnings, with five times
being average, it is. A short-term cut in your take of $50,000 per
year could bring $250,000 in an increased purchase price. And the
company will look more attractive at first blush, not just after
investigation. A profitable company is an easy sell—a borderline
one is much more difficult.

Understanding the Value of a Going Concern

If you understand the true value of your operating company, you
can price it more realistically and present it more enthusiastically.
It is always much easier to buy an existing business than to start
from scratch. If you are the founder, you should remember how
long it took and how much it cost before the company grew to a
breakeven level. You funded the start-up costs and the early losses.

A new owner will not have to go through this painful experience.
There is an existing revenue stream, dollars coming in the door
from the first day. If there are profits, there is payback on the

investment immediately. A start-up may not bring payback for years. This is the reason you are paid for assets and the value of a portion of future profits. You have put in your capital and your work to get here, now you are reaping the reward.

Revaluing Tangible Assets

There are times when the book value of your equipment is not reflective at all of its actual value. We are not talking about replacement costs here—you won't get near that amount. But if you know that some machines that are fully depreciated still have good resale value or that the rate at which you are depreciating major pieces of equipment is excessive, then perhaps you will wish to restate their value in a separate document. You must pay your accountant to prepare these documents, so be sure you'll get a return on that expense before you do the work.

Your own word will not be sufficient for this type of correction. You will have to hire an industrial appraiser, which can cost several thousand dollars. But if you are talking about a substantial difference in the asset's value, the cost might well be worth it. Also, if your buyer is looking for financing, this document could help that process because it adds to her asset base.

Once you have the appraiser's official assessment of the value of your equipment, do a restated balance sheet. This is by no means an official document, but it will form the basis for negotiation.

Selling to an Insider

The most likely buyer for your business may be in an office close to yours. Do you have a key employee who has been with you a long time and can manage the company almost as well as you can? Along the way, you should have had at least some conversation about a change of ownership, particularly if we are talking about a younger employee. If you have not yet had that conversation, you should have it as soon as you can.

It would be unfair and misunderstood if you put the business up for sale and never made an overture to a key employee who is interested. The important issue to consider is the value of the company, how much you need to get out of it, and whether this individual could muster the resources needed to buy it. If you know this is impossible, then you must have a full and honest discussion about it. If this is left unsaid and other buyers come forward, you could end up with a disgruntled key employee or one who resigns just when you need him the most.

If the deal is possible, you might be able to start very early by bonusing some shares of stock in return for loyalty and accomplishment. It is a good incentive. You could negotiate a formal buy-sell agreement long before it goes into effect, setting the value of the business at a benchmark based on results. When the time comes, all you would have to do is implement it.

A word of warning—these are tricky negotiations because you are close to this person. If the deal falls through, your working relationship may be damaged. At some point you both may want to turn the discussion over to representatives to avoid any personal misunderstandings. Each of you will eventually have an attorney in on the deal. Why not during the negotiations as well?

Using a Business Broker

Other than an insider, you may not have any other potential candidates. You may want to seek the services of a business broker firm. It may charge an up-front fee in order to "package" the business for sale. If you don't wish to do this work yourself, the fee, which can range from $2,500 to $10,000, may be worth it. The firm will normally base the fee on the selling price of the company (its potential for a commission) as well as on how much work will be required to market the company successfully. Don't pay a high up-front cost—commission is an incentive, fees may be less of one.

Understand that your broker's fees will usually be based on the entire sale price, not just the down payment. You can count on financing a portion—perhaps even a large part—of the sale price. So at closing you may get precious little money. For example, you sell for $200,000 with $50,000 down (25 percent). Your broker's commission is 15 percent and the firm gets $30,000 of the $50,000 at closing. The broker firm gets more money than you do! Ask about this in advance and negotiate terms that work for you. Tie the fee, in part, to your payment.

Selling the Company Yourself

If you cannot afford a broker, you may have to sell the company yourself. You may know more potential candidates than you think. Are there people within your industry who you know are working for others but have always seemed interested in ownership? There are a large number of mature middle managers, even bankers, being laid off, and some of them may want to be business owners. Don't broadcast your desire to sell; just put the word out that you are taking it under consideration. Talk with members of the business community, accountants, lawyers, and perhaps your banker (if this won't give away a secret you aren't ready to disclose to the bank). And don't forget your insurance agents, they are good business networkers.

A business actively for sale will change. The changes may be only subtle, but you may find management a bit more difficult. Your employees will know once lookers start walking around. Some may decide to leave rather than risk the unknown. Chances are, it won't be the underachievers who leave; they tend to stay. The performers who have more options are more likely to leave. At a time when you need to continue to have the best results, productivity could become a problem.

Suppliers may tighten credit when they get wind of the fact that your company is for sale. You may not get all of the special offerings and advantages once they realize that your tenure is short. And finally, customers may begin to change as well—finding a fallback position with new suppliers to protect themselves from unfavorable changes. Business could get soft as a result.

There is little you can do to head this off except be aware of it and try to spot problems before they happen. Talking an employee into staying or giving extra attention to a client might do the trick.

After the Deal: Getting Paid

The deal that you will make will have two parts—*how much* you will get paid and *how* you will get paid. You may readily understand the first part of the deal but you must also consider the second. Financing is a critical element of the deal. Here are four ways to finance an acquisition:

1. Publicly-traded stock in the acquiring company
2. Buyer's (individual) capital
3. Bank lending
4. Seller financing

The first option may seem the most secure but that isn't always true. It depends on the stability of the stock. Do your homework and track the performance of the stock. You may not be able to sell your holdings for some time and the prices may change dramatically. I am aware of one business purchase in 1997 that involved stock valued at $12/share, but before the buyer could begin to liquidate the shares, the stock had fallen to $3/share. What a loss!

Buyers should be required to invest their own capital into the deal. They will be more committed to success if they are at risk financially. A buyer with substantial capital may want a discount for a cash deal. It is something to consider because any money that is deferred is money at risk.

A combination of bank financing and buyer's capital is also possible. Few banks would be willing to lend 100 percent of the purchase price unless your buyer has substantial personal assets to pledge as collateral. Many times the deal will involve some owner financing as well. You should know that the bank's liens will be in front of yours so the bank will get paid ahead of you. And if there is any default, you will be struggling with the bank's attorneys over assets.

Seller financing at some level is very likely. It should *never* be for 100 percent of the purchase price. It isn't wise to turn over your assets to someone else for no consideration. The more up-front money you can get, the better. The balance should be a monthly payout over as short a period as you can negotiate. However, you know the cash flow realities of the business. Don't make a deal that seems unrealistic; it probably is and you won't get your money in a timely fashion.

Knowing When to Go

There is a beginning, a middle, and an end to a business career. If you work for someone else that is evident. In your own company, you set the rules—you can stay as long as you want. But the day will come when you want or need to get out. Plan for it, think about it, and then exit successfully.

CHAPTER

A Case Study

There are four basic cycles that small businesses go through over the life of the company and each has unique characteristics. Knowing where you are in this cycle will help you establish financial benchmarks to measure your progress and plan for the future.

Stage I—The Start-Up

In the beginning, new entrepreneurs tend to be overly optimistic about their ventures. Revenue projections are often much higher than actual results, and the budgets underestimate expenses so there is a need for more capital. Financial expertise is limited and outside resources and advisors are often not actively utilized. This results in a cash flow crisis that may be funded haphazardly from personal lines of credit, money borrowed from family and friends, or unpaid vendor credit.

Stage II—Growth

This is the period of real opportunity when the bulk of marketing is done and sales growth is at its highest level. The pressing need at this time is for capital to fund higher and higher levels of current assets, such as inventory and receivables. The establishment of a timely, flexible, and cost effective source of financing is critical to success at this stage.

Stage III—Maturation

Now the company will begin to bear the fruits of its labor with the availability of positive cash flow. Pressure can build from various stakeholders as to how competing goals will be met. Creditors (lenders as well as vendors) will expect to be paid, employees will expect improved compensation, and the owner will expect financial rewards for her previous risk and hard work.

The critical element here is to continue to allocate resources (human as well as capital) to the continued growth of the venture and to determine which exit strategy you will eventually pursue.

Stage IV—Transition

The business or current leadership may have gone past its prime in its present configuration, and serious self-assessment is required. The organization may need major restructuring as well as capital investment for new technology and/or new marketing.

The owner may want to exit to conserve personal capital, as this is often the time of greatest pressure to reinvest in the operation. Lenders are cautious about mature companies that lack serious strategies for the future.

The Start-Up

J.E. Industrial Distributing Company was started in 1977 by the top salesperson of another of Ohio's largest distribution companies. Jack Edmond (the owner) had grown to a 1976 personal sales volume in excess of $5 million, and he believed that most of his customers would follow him and purchase from his new company.

The gross profit margin of his original employer was 23 percent with a direct cost of 77 percent of goods, based on prices delivered to its warehouse. Jack based his original start-up budgets and pro forma statement on these assumptions, which ultimately turned out to be overly optimistic. His business plan and loan request for $400,000 included the following financial estimates:

Start-Up Budget

Inventory	$600,000[1]
Leasehold improvements	35,000[2]
Trucks (2)	25,000[3]
Shelving	10,000
Office equipment	20,000
Working capital	200,000[4]
Total required	$890,000

Jack also identified his sources of capital as follows:

Owner's investment	$150,000
Vendor credit	140,000
Bank loan	600,000
Total required	$890,000

[1]Based on $400,000 month in volume—this was 45 days inventory.

[2]Converting a portion of the warehouse into offices.

[3]Two used step vans for delivery.

[4]Expected overhead for first 90 days.

His first year pro forma projected the following:

Quarter:	1	2	3	4	
Sales income	$1,000,000	$1,000,000	$1,200,000	$1,200,000	
Cost of sales	770,000	770,000	924,000	924,000	77%
Gross profit	230,000	230,000	286,000	286,000	23%
General & administrative expense					
Rent	12,000	12,000	12,000	12,000	
Salaries[1]	26,700	26,700	26,700	26,700	
Office expense	15,000	15,000	15,000	15,000	
Telephone	10,500	10,500	10,500	10,500	
Utilities	1,500	1,500	1,500	1,500	
Travel/ entertainment	15,000	15,000	15,000	15,000	
Marketing	4,500	4,500	4,500	4,500	
Interest[2]	18,000	18,000	18,000	18,000	
Owner's draw	21,000	21,000	21,000	21,000	
Total Cost	124,200	124,200	124,200	124,200	12%
Profit (before tax)	$ 105,800	$ 105,800	$ 161,800	$ 161,800	

[1]Staff included receptionist, bookkeeper, warehouse worker, truck driver, and second salesperson at a $3,000/month draw

[2]Twelve percent on $600,000

The reality for J.E. Industrial Distributing was far different from the one assumed. There were two major miscalculations. The first was in the area of revenue. The first year's volume was only 60 percent of the amount that was projected. The reality was that a number of customers remained with their original supplier, in part due to contractual relationships. The second was that the gross profit margin was actually 19 percent instead of 23 percent. This was due to higher direct costs from manufacturers based on a lower volume of purchases. The first year's actual results looked like this:

Quarter	1	2	3	4	
Sales income	$600,000	$600,000	$750,000	$750,000	
Cost of sales	486,000	486,000	607,500	607,500	81%
Gross profit	114,000	114,000	142,500	142,500	19%
General & administrative expense:					
Rent	12,000	12,000	12,000	12,000	
Salaries	26,700	26,700	26,700	26,700	
Office expense	15,000	15,000	15,000	15,000	
Telephone	10,500	10,500	10,500	10,500	
Utilities	1,500	1,500	1,500	1,500	
Travel/entertainment	15,000	15,000	15,000	15,000	
Marketing	14,500	14,500	7,500	7,500	
Interest	18,000	18,000	18,000	18,000	
Owner's draw	21,000	21,000	21,000	21,000	
Total cost	134,200	134,200	127,200	127,200	
Overhead as % of sales	20%	20%	18%	18%	
Profit (loss)	$(19,800)	$(19,800)	$ 15,300	$ 15,300	

Total loss for the year was $9,000.

At the end of one year in business, the company was experiencing tight cash flow for a number of reasons. The primary cause was that it overpurchased new inventory, expecting a higher volume of sales and expecting some contracts that did not materialize. Sales of $300,000 to $400,000 per month would have required inventory approximately double that amount. But with sales of $200,000 per month, the starting inventory was excessive and strangled cash flow. In addition, customer payments were slower than anticipated, so cash was often short and vendor bills were often extended past 60 days. Suppliers had been very patient. While owners' compensation was deferred when necessary, it was expensed to account for the full cost of Jack's wages. His draw from his previous employer was 30 percent higher; the current level represented 3 percent of actual sales, which had been his commission rate as a salesperson.

The balance sheet at the end of year one looked like this:

Cash in banks	$ 21,400
Accounts receivable	365,000
Inventory	571,000
Prepaid insurance	19,000
Utility deposits	2,500
Total current assets	978,900
Vehicles	25,000
Leaseholds	35,000
	60,000
less depreciation	9,000
	51,000
Total assets	1,029,900
Liabilities—current	
Accounts payable	566,700
Deferred wages	37,000
Notes payable—current portion	110,000
Total current liabilities	713,700
Long-term portion of loan	
Total liabilities	300,000
	1,013,700
Common stock	25,000
Retained earnings	(9,000)
Net equity	16,000
Total liabilities and capital	$1,029,600

For a start-up venture, this balance sheet is not bad, particularly because the current ratios show solvency, yet they do reflect the tight cash situation. Current assets had a ratio of 1.3-to-1 which is a bit low but not unreasonable for a start-up. Aggressive collection of receivables and higher turnover of inventory kept the operation moving, and most vendors were cooperative because they had great optimism for the venture. Higher volume also would lead to higher purchasing levels and lower net costs with volume discounts and prepaid freight.

Sales were the key issue, and resources were committed to growth. Additional money was allocated to marketing. The first breakthrough came at the end of year two when sales were up to $3 million and operations were comfortably profitable. J.E. Industrial Distributing was about to be awarded a 1.5 million dollar contract that would put it at its goal in profitability. The only problem was how to finance the additional business.

Getting Ready for Growth

Year two had been a successful one in tightening up the balance sheet, a necessity if new capital was to be secured. The company was only two years into the original loan and now the need was for a revolving line of credit to finance growth.

Year two balance sheet looked like this:

Cash in banks	$ 45,000	
Accounts receivable	405,000	
Inventory	400,000	
Prepaid insurance	12,000	
Utility deposits	1,500	
Total current assets	863,500	(1)
Vehicles	25,000	
Leaseholds	35,000	
Total	60,000	
less depreciation	18,000	
	42,000	
Total assets	$905,500	

Liabilities—current		
Accounts payable	$395,000	
Deferred wages	21,000	
Notes payable—current portion	110,000	
Total current liabilities	526,000	(2)
Long-term portion of loan	202,000	
Total liabilities	728,000	
Common stock	25,000	
Retained earnings	152,500	
Net equity	177,500	
Total liabilities and capital	$905,500	

Note the current assets (1) at $863,500 and current liabilities (2) at $526,000. Now the ratio was at about 1.6-to-1 (1.6 of asset for every 1 of liability), which was a substantial improvement—sure to impress any banker. This was achieved by reducing inventory levels and putting the capital directly into lowering payables. The business was running far more efficiently. Vendors were being paid more promptly and everything was in place for securing additional financing.

New sales of approximately $150,000 per month were expected, requiring at least 60 days inventory of $240,000 (based on 80 percent cost of two months sales of $300,000). These sales would become receivables and turn into cash, so a revolving line of credit for $300,000 would be more than enough to fund this growth. The increased purchasing power would also lower unit costs, and profits would meet the 23 percent original projection. The sales and gross profit volume were also likely to meet the start-up pro forma. However, by now the overhead costs were higher and the net profit lower.

The third year results were the following:

Sales	$4,600,000	
Cost of sales	3,522,000	77%
Gross profit	1,078,000	
General and administrative expense		
Rent	60,000	
Salaries[1]	300,000	
Office expense[2]	90,000	
Telephone	35,000	
Utilities	9,000	
Travel/entertainment[3]	72,000	
Marketing	50,000	
Interest	65,000	
Owner's draw	150,000	
Miscellaneous[4]	40,000	
Total administrative cost	871,000	
Profit (before tax)	$ 207,000	4.6%

[1]Staffing levels had increased to three administrative staff, two truck drivers, and two outside salespeople.

[2]Office expense included outside contractors (including a payroll service) and purchase of a computer system, which was expensed.

[3]Travel to all major conventions were now budgeted and all salespeople had entertainment budgets.

[4]This included employee benefits and truck expense.

J.E.'s Breakeven Point

By year three, Jack felt that he had an excellent sense of what it took to operate his company efficiently. The staff and overhead cost that he had budgeted for year three had been well thought out and appeared reasonable. Operating costs of $870,000 were used to determine breakeven volume.

At a 23 percent gross profit margin, sales of $3.7 million generated operating profits of $860,000, which was the breakeven target. With current sales of almost $1 million over this number, J.E.'s financial health was solid.

The next few years were spent working on enlarging the customer base, but this resulted in little actual growth—new business was mostly replacing old business that was lost.

The Mature Company

For four years, J.E. seemed to run very efficiently. Sales volume was slightly under $5 million, cash flow was positive, and everyone seemed satisfied—including the bank that had its first loan retired in a timely manner. However, overhead costs were going up with everyone costing "just a bit" more. The salespeople now had cars, Jack's draw had gone to $180,000 annually, and some of his personal expenses were covered by the company.

Overhead had increased by $100,000, although this had not reflected totally on net (before tax) profits. The difference was made up by a slightly higher gross margin created by better purchasing skills.

The company seemed on solid footing until a massive change in market conditions in the mid-1980s. A serious recession in the Midwestern industrial market dropped sales dramatically over a six-month period, with many of the losses permanent as customers shuttered parts of their operations. At the end of the slide, sales were off by 30 percent and now registered annually at $3.5 million. With overhead now at $970,000, the outcomes were substantially changed as follows:

Sales	$3,500,000	
Cost of goods	2,695,000	77%
Gross profit	805,000	
Less overhead	970,000	
Profit (loss)	$ (165,000)	

This eight-year-old company was in a serious struggle for survival. The major focus became cost cutting and a strict budgeting process. Everyone realized that the breakeven point had to be lowered to below $800,000 in order to reduce the losses at the lower current volume. It is also possible to raise margins in some companies by lowering direct costs. This was not an option for J.E. because its material costs were as low as they could be. In fact, because costs were tied to volume buying, it was difficult to keep them from rising as volume dropped. Much of the working capital had dried up in funding the losses. The bank let J.E. draw down the full amount of its line of credit, but would not entertain any new financing until the situation changed. Tight inventory management was crucial to this process.

Making a Transition

In 1991, J.E. Industrial Distributing made a very critical decision for its future. Three years of aggressive selling effort had shown less than $1 million of new sales; profits were back, but they remained small. More volume was the only answer.

Another specialty distribution company whose sales had also dropped in the mid 1980s and not come back was facing the same problem. Its sales seemed stuck at $5.5 million. The two companies merged.

The results were quick and dramatic. The consolidation cut overhead for each one by almost 40 percent—office and warehouse space was shared, as was administrative staff. Two trucks were all they needed together and one salesperson was cut. The combined volume of $9 million was achieved with surprisingly low overhead and resulted in before-tax profits of almost 6 percent. Growth to this day has remained slow but steady and the partnership has been a win for both.

Glossary

Accounts Payable are all outstanding debts to vendors. A listing of accounts payable is normally compiled alphabetically and the entries are made by the date of the invoice. Vendor credit may be a significant portion of working capital so due dates must be tracked for payment. Some suppliers charge a penalty if not paid within certain terms. At the end of each month, accounts payable should be aged in a report showing amount due and age of all monies due.

Accounts Payable Turnover is calculated by dividing total purchase dollars by current total **accounts payable.** The ratio may be divided into 365 to give the average number of days it takes the company to pay a vendor invoice.

Accounts Receivable are the money due from all customers currently owing at least one invoice to the company. The total of these invoices is shown on the balance sheet as an asset. Accounts receivable should be aged in a report at the end of each month as they represent expected incoming **cash flow.**

Accounts Receivable Turnover is figured when the total dollars of sales are divided by the total dollars of **accounts receivable.** This number divided into 365 will show the number of days required to turn a sale (including credit) into cash. Accounts receivable turnover is a benchmark number for measuring the effectiveness of collection policy.

Accrual Base Accounting reflects income that is recognized at the time a sale is made, rather than when payment is due. Expense is recognized at the time it is incurred, rather than when it is paid. Revenue and expense are matched during a fixed accounting period, allowing for accurate comparisons.

Balance Sheet shows the summary of assets and **liabilities** of a company. It is created at the end of an accounting period such as a month, a quarter, or a year. Subtracting liabilities from assets shows the **net worth** of the business. Assets are listed as current or fixed and liabilities are listed as current or long term.

Book Value is the value of any asset shown on the **balance sheet.** It is determined by the item's cost and then reduced by the amount of **depreciation.** The book value of an item does not necessarily reflect its current market value. Accelerated depreciation may reduce the value below market.

Business Plan is a written document describing the nature of the business, the sales and marketing strategy, and the financial background, and containing a projected **profit and loss statement.** Originally written as a strategic plan for a new business, it should be updated every year and revamped every three years.

Cash Basis Accounting is a system that recognizes income only when the money is received, and expense only after payment is made. This works best for a business where most transactions are done with cash instead of credit. There is no match of revenue against expense in a fixed accounting period, so comparisons of previous periods are not possible. There is less financial control on a cash basis system.

Cash Flow is the difference between the available cash at the beginning of an accounting period and that at the end of a period. Cash comes in from sales, loan proceeds, investments, and sale of assets. It flows out to pay for operating and direct expenses, principal **debt service,** and the purchase of assets.

Cash Flow Statement measures the inflow of revenue versus the outflow of expense. The most relevant type of cash flow statement is done on an operating basis. You may also include loan proceeds once it has been established that they will be forthcoming.

Collateral consists of any tangible assets that are pledged and encumbered to secure a loan.

Chart of Accounts is a numerical listing of all items contained in the financial statement of a company, including assets, **liabilities,** income, and expense.

Current Assets are those assets that are in cash or are expected to be turned into cash within one year, such as **inventory** and **accounts receivable.** Cash assets will not include any miscellaneous **payables** such as notes from officers because there may be no expectation that they will be paid on any specific schedule.

Current Liabilities are debts or costs that are due within one year. These include **accounts payable;** current portions due of any loans; and any accrued but unpaid items such as taxes, insurance, or benefits such as accrued vacation pay.

Current Ratios compare current assets to current **liabilities.** There should be about twice as many assets as liabilities, for a 2-to-1 ratio, to ensure sufficient **cash flow** to meet obligations (also called solvency).

Debt is money owed to a lender, vendor, service provider, or any other creditor.

Debt Service is the complete payment of an obligation, including principal and interest.

Debt-to-Equity Ratio is calculated by dividing **debt** by **equity.** If ratios are increasing—more debt in relation to equity—the company is being financed by creditors rather than by internal positive cash flow. This may be a dangerous trend.

Depreciation is an expense item set up to express the diminishing life expectancy and value of any equipment (including vehicles). Depreciation is set up over a fixed period of time based on current tax regulations. Items fully depreciated are no longer carried as assets on the company books.

Direct Costs are the costs of material and labor that are directly attributable to the level of sales or production, and may also include the costs of direct subcontractors. Direct costs are referred to as variable costs because they rise as volume increases and drop as it decreases. Total revenue less direct costs equals the **gross profit** from operations.

Equity, also called net worth, is the difference between the total assets of the business and the total **liabilities.** Shown on the liability side of the **balance sheet,** equity may be thought of as an amount owed to owners because theoretically it would be disbursed to them if assets were sold and liabilities paid.

Fixed Expenses are the overhead costs that are constant regardless of the level of sales.

Gross Profit is derived from the gross (total before paying taxes) sales revenue less any direct costs such as labor, material, and subcontracting that is directly attributable to those sales.

    Also referred to as operating profits, the gross profit represents the money available to pay **overhead** expenses and taxes, and to generate a **net profit** for the company to retain as **working capital.**

Income Statement is a document generated monthly and/or annually that defines the earnings of a company by stating all relevant income and all expenses that have been generated by that income. Also referred to as a **profit and loss statement.**

Indirect Costs are expenses not directly related to sales, and include items such as rent and utilities, plus administrative **overhead** including office salaries, professional fees, and selling expenses. Indirect costs are called overhead or **fixed expenses** because they continue regardless of the sales level of the company.

Inventory consists of the assets held for sale, which may include finished goods, work in progress, and raw material. When valuing work in progress, the added value of direct labor involved in producing the finished product may increase the real worth of inventory, yet may not be realized until the work is complete and the goods are released to the customer.

Inventory Turnover is a ratio calculated by dividing the total costs of material in costs of goods sold by the current **inventory.** Decreasing ratios (fewer turnovers per year) may indicate that there are slow selling items in current inventory, which put pressure on the cash position because they will not turn to cash in the current cycle.

Labor Costs are divided into two types—direct and indirect. Direct labor costs are related to producing products and performing services. Indirect labor costs are related to the work involved in distribution, sales, and the administrative duties involved on operating the business. Labor costs include any taxes and benefits due as a result of the payment of wages.

Liability is money that is owed to a lender or other creditor, and is an effect of any owed assets.

Line of Credit is an instrument of credit issued by a bank or other lender for short-term (usually one year) capital needs. Most lines are revolving; that is, they can be drawn down, repaid, and drawn on again. A nonrevolving line may be drawn only once.

A line of credit should be paid to zero at least once during the year as its purpose is short-term financing of **inventory** and receivables. While a line of credit is granted for one year, it may be renewed on a regular basis.

Liquidity is the ability to pay obligations as they become due, using cash on hand or cash generated from the normal turnover (sale) of **inventory** and from the collection of receivables. Long-term assets (property and equipment) are not measured because they provide no cash from which to retire current **debts** unless they are sold outright and become cash items.

Net Profit is the amount of money earned after all expenses (often with the exception of taxes) are deducted.

Net Worth is the amount of **equity** a company has, which is the difference between the total assets and the total **liabilities.**

Overhead is the **indirect costs** or **fixed expenses** of operating the business, ranging from rent to administrative costs to marketing costs. The majority of these costs stay fixed (the amount is the same from month to month) regardless of sales volume, although a few that are sales-associated may be considered semivariable.

Payables is a list that includes the amount of money owed to all creditors.

Profit and Loss Statement is often prepared monthly and/or quarterly, and always annually. This statement reports income and expenses, and the results are expressed as a profit or loss. The report identifies by category all income, whether from the sales of products or services or from other activities; it reports all **direct** and **indirect costs.** Operating (**gross** or after-tax) **profits** are listed as are the **net** (before tax) **profit.**

Pro forma is a preliminary report that may be created as both a **profit and loss statement** and a **cash flow statement.** A pro forma for an existing company is a prediction of financial results in future periods, based in part on historical happenings and in part on anticipated new income or expenses. A pro forma is also created for a new enterprise in order to project future capital needs.

Rate of Interest (Fixed or Variable) determines how much interest you must pay on a loan and how the loan is paid off. The interest rate that is in effect at the start of a loan may not always be the interest charged throughout the life of the loan. Only a fixed rate loan has one rate during the entire term, which normally is limited to five years or less. The only long-term loans that are fixed are mortgages, and these loans are sold off through Fannie Mae or Freddie Mac, which relieves the bank of the interest rate risk.

A variable rate loan has a floating rate pegged to an index, such as the prime rate, and goes up and down according to that rate. Some loans may have semifixed rates for one year, and then they float; they also may have a minimum (floor) as well as a maximum (ceiling).

Retained Earnings are profits that are not distributed through dividends but are left in the business and carried on the books. This amount is reduced over time by any losses.

Secured Loan has assets pledged as **collateral** that may be liquidated if the loan is not paid according to the agreement.

Uniform Commercial Code (UCC) When a lender wishes to perfect its secured interest in certain assets, it may do so in a number of ways. One is to take possession as with stocks and bonds that are held as security. Another is to file an encumbrance on a title such as that of a vehicle. Where there are a variety of assets in the possession and control of the borrower, the lender will file a Uniform Commercial Code financing statement with the secretary of state where the borrower is located. These financing statements are normally signed by the borrower at the time the loan closes.

Unsecured Loan is a loan that has no underlying **collateral** pledged to the lender to offset any losses in case of default. An unsecured loan normally carries a higher interest rate than a loan secured by collateral.

Venture Capital consists of funds flowing into a company in the form of an investment rather than a loan. Controlled by an individual or a small group known as venture capitalists, these investments require a high rate of return and they are secured by a substantial ownership position in the business. Equity interest transfers back to the original owners when all loan payments and/or premiums are paid.

Working Capital is the difference between **current assets** and **current liabilities;** it is an indication of **liquidity** and the ability of the company to meet current obligations. The assumption is that current assets will turn into cash concurrently with obligations such as payables and loans coming due.

The variable here is the collectability of current receivables and the salability of inventory. Failure of either may mean that a company is less liquid in reality than it appears to be on paper.

Working Capital Ratio is calculated by dividing **current assets** by **current liabilities.** A decreasing ratio indicates that working capital is being reduced by losses such as the purchase of long-term assets or distribution to owners. This ratio may be used to compare your company with peer companies and to monitor trends.

Index